LOOKING BACK
at
NORFOLK
CRICKET

by PHILIP YAXLEY

NOSTALGIA
Publications

TOFTWOOD · DEREHAM · NORFOLK

Published by:
NOSTALGIA PUBLICATIONS
(Terry Davy)
7 Elm Park, Toftwood,
Dereham, Norfolk, NR19 1NB

First Impression 1997

ISBN 0 947630 16 3

Design and Typesetting:
NOSTALGIA PUBLICATIONS

Printed by:
COLOURPRINT
Fakenham, Norfolk

Front cover and title page illustration: Fuller Pilch 1804-1870

CONTENTS

This book reflects how over two hundred years a Minor County has enjoyed some "First-Class" cricket.

The book is dedicated to Evergreens Norman Brighton and Eddie Symonds, who have loved their cricket through many decades.

Looking back at Norfolk cricket - Norman and Eddie peruse an old score-book

Foreword
by John Edrich, M.B.E.

As cricket has been played in Norfolk for over 200 years, I am sure this book of photographs and pictures, compiled by Philip Yaxley, will be of great interest to all those cricket lovers in the County of Norfolk and to many other followers of cricket throughout the country.

For my part I was very fortunate to have been born into a cricketing family; I learnt to play the great game on the lovely village greens and club grounds that are abundant throughout the County.

Although Norfolk has never been a first-class cricket county, it has over the years produced several cricketers who played the game at the highest level.

I have had a wonderful life through cricket and I am sure that, when you read this book, many of you will have very happy memories of games gone by.

John Edrich

John Edrich

John Edrich is a cricket legend. He played for Surrey between 1958 and 1978 and throughout his career was a most dependable left-handed opening batsman. His 39,790 first-class runs were made at an average of 45.47 and he is one of that small band of all-time greats who have made a hundred first-class centuries.

In 77 Test appearances for England, John scored 5,138 runs at an average of 43.54, his top score being a monumental 310 not out against New Zealand at Headingley in 1965.

Before going to the Oval he had captained the Bracondale School XI, as well as playing for the likes of South Walsham and Norwich C.E.Y.M.S. He turned out for Norfolk in 1954 and, after leaving Surrey, again in 1979.

Recent years have seen involvement in the England set-up as batting coach. His own innings were always characterised by grit and determination, no more so than when he played for his country. The award of the M.B.E. in the 1977 Birthday Honours was richly deserved.

Chapter One

The Early Years

A boy cricketer captured by Cleer Alger (Junior),
the Diss photographer, between 1865-75

In The Beginning

THIS advertisement, which appeared in the "Norwich Mercury" in May 1745, is the first reference in the local press to cricket in the County. By the 1760s among the leading teams were Diss, Great Yarmouth, Norwich, Shipdham and Swaffham. Great rivalry ensued between Swaffham and the powerful Shipdham team,

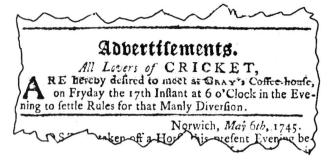

who, around 1770, were issuing challenges to any town side in the County and even "All Norfolk". Soon clubs like Brinton, Castle Acre, Docking, East Dereham, Holt and Wells were playing the game. In 1789, when Castle Acre triumphed by an innings and four runs in a return encounter with Docking, it was recorded that Docking "have been a number of years the champions of this County". At that time the game was particularly strong in North Norfolk.

The first mention of a County match was in 1764 when the Gentlemen of Norfolk defeated those of Suffolk at Bury St. Edmunds. A further game between the sides was staged on Dickleburgh Moor in 1781.

A contemporary engraving of the game played at Swaffham Racecourse between 33 players of Norfolk and an All-England XI in July 1797. Described at the time as "the greatest Cricket Match ever played in this County", the epic encounter was contested for a purse of 500 guineas. The England XI boasted most of the finest cricketers of the day, among them the all-rounder John Hammond, who kept wicket, Thomas Walker, a great defensive bat, and the legendary William Beldham.

Spectators flocked to Swaffham for the game and many of the nobility journeyed there from London and elsewhere. Some days before the event, it was reported that beds at the inns and private houses were "mostly engaged". However, as the accompanying scorecard shows, the Norfolk 33 were thrashed by an innings and 13 runs, Tom Walker's 55 outscoring the whole of the County's first innings.

A further match took place between elevens raised by the 9th Earl of Winchelsea and Lord Beauclerk, many of the nobility participating. Appearing in Lord Beauclerk's side was the immortal Thomas Lord, the founder of Lord's Cricket Ground, who had spent some of his childhood at Diss.

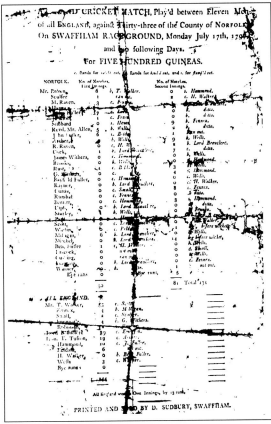

Born at Horningtoft, Norfolk, in 1804, Fuller Pilch was only 17 when he first appeared at Lord's in 1820 for the County against the Marylebone Club. However, on this occasion it was the home side's William Ward who stole the show by scoring 278, the highest single innings at the time. After a spell with the Bury St. Edmunds Club in the mid-1820s Pilch went on to become England's top batsman. Employing a short-handled bat, he relied on forward play.

In much-publicised single wicket contests in 1833, he defeated Yorkshire's hero Tom Marsden, first at Norwich and then before over 12,000 spectators at Sheffield. The following year Pilch scored 87 not out and 73 in totals of 216 and 191 in a Norfolk victory over Yorkshire, while in the uncompleted return match, which Yorkshire claimed, he was 153 not out in the second innings.

An offer of a salary of £100 per annum saw him leave to enjoy a long career with Kent, and he died at Canterbury in 1870.

A scoresheet (right) of a match in which Holt entertained and were beaten by the mighty Nottingham team in 1821. The game was played on "beautifully prepared turf" at Holt Heath and "the arrangement of booths, marquees, flags, streamers, etc." was first-class.

With Fuller Pilch, together with his brothers Nathaniel and William, in the side, Holt were considered at the time to be the top club among those from Cambridgeshire, Norfolk and Suffolk. However, Nottingham were superior in batting and they won the return game a year later by 105 runs. By the mid-1820s several of Holt's young stars, including Fuller Pilch, had moved on and the club lost its superiority in local cricketing circles.

PARTICULARS OF A
Grand Cricket Match,
Between 11 of Nottingham Club, and 11 of Holt Club, Norfolk.
Which commenced on Monday, July 30, 1821.

For 120 Guineas aside.

Holt First Innings.

Charles Brunton,	0	Hit the Wicket.	F. Pilch,	8	Not out.	
W. Englebright,	6	Run out.	R. Englebright,	8	Bowled by Barker.	
R. J. Brereton,	6	Bowled by Hopkin.	J. Carmichael,	0	Ditto.	
Wm. Pilch,	14	Do. by Barker.	Robert Frost,	2	Ditto.	
Nathaniel Pilch,	21	Run out.	Wm. Goggs,	0	Ditto.	
Jno. Garwood,	6	Bowled by Hopkin.			Byes, 3—Total 80.	

Nottingham First Innings.

Geo. Thorpe,	3	Ct. by R. Englebright.	C. Jarvis,	10	Caught by Goggs.
George Jarvis,	11	Bowled by W. Pilch.	T. Barker,	0	Ditto by Brunton.
Joseph Dennis,	31	Ditto.	J. Hewitt,	24	Not out.
W. Clarke,	7	Ditto by F. Pilch.	P. Brambley,	21	Run out.
H. Hopkin,	4	Ditto.	J. Britain,	0	Bowled by F. Pilch.
G. Smith,	28	Ditto.			Byes, 11—Total 150.

Holt Second Innings.

Charles Brunton,	1	Bowled by Barker.	F. Pilch,	0	Bowled by Clarke.
W. Englebright,	10	Caught by Brambly.	R. Englebright,	8	Ditto.
R. Brereton,	0	Bowled by Clarke.	John Carmichael,	1	Caught by C. Jarvis
Wm. Pilch,	11	Ditto.	R. Frost,	25	Bowled by Barker
N. Pilch,	12	Ditto Barker.	Wm. Goggs,	3	Not out.
John Garwood	5	Caught by Dennis			Byes 9—Total 73.

Nottingham Second Innings.

Joseph Dennis,	2	Not out-
H. Hopkin,	2	Ditto-
	Total 4—Majority 1.	

Eleven Wickets to go down.

S. BARBER, Printer, Nottingham.

Cricket Match.
On Monday July 22nd, 1839,
A CRICKET MATCH
WILL BE PLAYED AT
Thetford,
On the COMMON, near the UNION-HOUSE,
Between Eleven Gentlemen of the Mildenhall Club, and Eleven Gentlemen of the Thetford Club.

WICKETS TO BE PITCHED AT TEN O'CLOCK.

R. Carley, Printer, Thetford.

RULES
OF THE
THETFORD CRICKET CLUB.

1st.—That there be a Committee of 6 Members, consisting of a President, Treasurer, Secretary and 3 others, who shall be elected at the first meeting, and that 3 form a quorum.

2nd.—Subscription to be 10s., to be paid on entry, to the Treasurer or one of the Committee.

3rd.—That the Secretary shall have the power of calling a General Meeting, when deemed necessary for the Business of the Club.

4th.—Any Member misconducting himself in any way, shall be expelled the Club by a majority, at any General Meeting.

5th.—That the Committee shall have the power of accepting any new Member.

6th.—That the Committee have the power of choosing the eleven or elevens, to play in Matches, Umpires and Scorers, and that all financial and other matters be under their absolute control.

7th.—That any Member whose subscription be unpaid within one month, after notice from the Secretary, shall be no longer considered a Member of the Club.

8th.—That the days of playing will be Mondays and Fridays, at 4 o'Clock.

9th.—The Second Monday in every Month to be a Field-day, play to commence at 2 o'Clock.

10th.—That all disputes respecting the Game of Cricket, be decided by the Marylebone Rules.

11th.—That if any Member being chosen by the Committee, and agreeing to play in a match, shall neglect to do so, (except in case of illness or any other cause satisfactory to the Committee,) he shall forfeit five shillings.

12th.—That on the first Monday in September, there shall be a general meeting, at which the Treasurer shall exhibit his accounts for the inspection and approval of the Members.

14th.—That no Rule of this Club shall be altered or expunged, except by the vote of a majority of members present, after a week's notice.

16th.—That any Member refusing to comply with these Rules, shall be expelled from the Club.

W. P. SALTER, Esq., President.
E. HOUGHEN, Esq., Treasurer.
G. W. MACKENZIE, Esq., Secretary.

R. CARLEY, PRINTER, KING-STREET, THETFORD.

The match advertised in this handbill (above) resulted in a win for Mildenhall by just four runs. Afterwards "the members and a party of gentlemen in the town dined together at the White Hart Inn, Thetford".

By the mid-19th century clubs like Thetford, which was reformed in 1844, were being established on a formal basis with sets of rules like those on page 10. The Lynn club had published its Rules in 1833.

Moves were made in 1826 to form the Norfolk County Cricket Club and its officers were elected at a meeting in January 1827. From its 1835 Rules, number 21 makes interesting reading. By 1831 Norfolk C.C.C. was being described as "now the next club to Marylebone" and it was regularly playing, and sometimes beating, the likes of M.C.C. and Yorkshire. At the outset Herbert Jenner was Norfolk's top player and by the early 1830s Pilch was excelling. In 1848 the club folded, was revived again in 1862, and then collapsed for about six years in 1870.

19th.—That all subscriptions shall be paid into Messrs. Gurney's Bank, or to the Treasurers.

20th.—That all disputes respecting the *Game of Cricket* shall be decided by the Marylebone Rules.

21st.—That all Members, Clergymen excepted, shall be requested to wear an uniform dress at the annual Meetings, to be as follows :—A dark blue coat, with buttons lettered *N. C. C.* and the motto of the Club. The buttons to be procured at Mr. Etheridge's, Jeweller, Norwich; and no buttons differing in the slightest particular from those sold by him shall be considered the buttons of the *N. C. C.*

Pages from the "Register of Cricket for Hingham by An Old Player", which was compiled by Thomas Driver and published in 1844. It recorded the performances of the mid-Norfolk club from 1802 to 1842.

Twice in 1829 Hingham defeated the County Club and in the same year also beat Norwich. At that time it was Dereham, Litcham, Swaffham and Hingham who were "celebrated for the skill of their cricketers".

The year 1815 saw an extraordinary match, played on Hempton Green, between the united parishes of Litcham, Dunham and Brisley, and those of Walsingham and Fakenham. The latter team, "although unparalleled in the annals of cricketing", did not score a single run!

24

In the latter part of this season a game was played at Hingham with Attleborough club.

ATTLEBOROUGH.	1st inns.	2nd do.	HINGHAM.	1st inns.	2nd do.
Etheridge	9	0	Bilham	0	0
Goldspink	16	2	Yeomans	0	0
Wilson	0	0	Waller	0	2
Cushing	11	2	Hands	0	0
Francklin	1	2	Semmence	10	9
Smith	13	5	W. Roberts	2	12
Rose	11	1	Cowles	2	6
Upston	7	19	Driver, jun.	25	2
Palmer	9	0	Stafford	10	0
Brothers	0	1	Webster	0	7
Dalney	0	0	Skippon	6	0
Byes	4	2	Byes	3	2
Wide	10	3			
	91	39		86	58
	30			58	
	130			144	

Thus Hingham having the majority by 14 runs.
The bowling on either sides was not as good as usual, Ashby one of the Hingham bowlers being absent, playing in another match.
The return match was played at the town of Attleborough, when Hingham again came off conquerors by a very large number of runs.—Score.

HINGHAM.	1st inns.	2nd do.	ATTLEBOROUGH.	1st inns.	2nd do.
W. Roberts	68	26	Richard Goldspink	0	0
Waller	5	1	Palmer	0	0
Semmence	0	1	Cushing	4	4
Skipper	0	2	Upston	0	5
Driver	0	3	Wilson	7	6
Cowles	7	0	Rose	1	3
Bilham	0	3	Smith	0	6
Howard	1	6	Brothers	4	2
Ashby	6	0	Dawes	0	0
Yeoman	2	0	Etheridge	0	0
Stafford	10	5	Francklin, Esq.	0	0
Wide	4	1	Wide	5	5
Byes	1	1	Byes	0	3
			No balls		1
	115	59		33	35
	59			35	
	172			68	
	104			68	

This indeed was a very hollow match, the batting of Mr. W. Roberts was superb, scoring 94, an immense number.
Although the Att'boro' came so near in the first game, it is quite certain they never were able to match themselves with Hingham.

25

1843.

The first match played by Hingham this year was with Harling. The following is the score.

HINGHAM.	1st inns.	2nd do.	HARLING.	1st inns.	2nd do
Mr. J. Tallent	0	3	Mr. J. Smith	0	16
Yeomans	10	3	Bailey	2	1
Cowles	13	0	Cawthorn	0	7
Semmence	4	20	J. Daines	0	6
Waller	14	1	Wickers	4	4
Howard	5	7	T. Daines	4	2
Francklin, Esq.	5	0	Houchin	2	0
W. Roberts	6	14	S. Smith	1	8
W. Ashby	0	13	Betts	0	0
F. Alexander	2	12	J. Kerrison	1	0
J. Nicholson	1	2	Barber	2	0
Byes and Wide	4	4	Byes and Wide	8	11
	63	79		31	50
	62				31
	141				81

This was their first victory this year, which was a glorious season for Hingham, winning eight matches without losing one. Dereham 2, Harling 2, Shipdham 2, Bungay 2. The Hingham side at this time was very strong, several young players having entered this year.
The return match was played at Harling, and again won by the Hingham.

HINGHAM.	1st inns.	2nd inns.	HARLING.	1st inns.	2nd inns.
Mr. W. Roberts	1	29	Mr. Arnold	2	5
Waller	12	0	Bailey	0	0
Semmence	0	0	Daines	13	0
Cowles	1	0	Wickes	7	5
F. Alexander	0	0	G. Kerrison	3	1
Howard	0	11	J. Kerrison	1	2
Francklin	0	9	Betts	2	0
Yeomans	5	2	Watson	2	0
Nicholson	5	2	Cawthorn	2	0
Ashby	0	12	Wright	0	0
Driver, jun.	3	1	Smith	0	0
Byes and Wide	10	12	Kerrison	1	2
			Wide and Byes	5	9
	42	70		37	24
		42			37
	112				61

The Harling were allowed Arnold, an excellent bowler from Cambridge.

9

Gunton Park

THESE pictures of the I. Zingari and Gentlemen of Norfolk teams, which met at Gunton Park in September 1862, are probably the earliest surviving photographs relating to Norfolk cricket in existence. In a low-scoring game I. Zingari, the famous wandering club, defeated the County team by six wickets.

I. Zingari

Pictured sitting in the middle at the front with I. Zingari is Lord Suffield, a great patron of Norfolk cricket. On the same photograph, the bearded player holding a bat and leaning against a pillar is R. A. Fitzgerald, the mid-Victorian Secretary of M.C.C. Among other great centres

Gentlemen of Norfolk

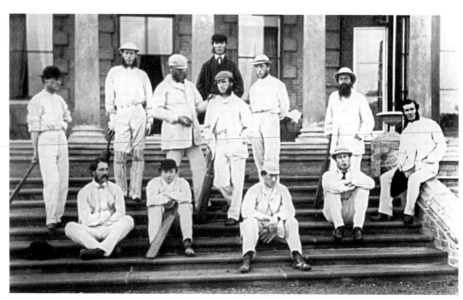

of country-house cricket were Blickling, Holkham and Houghton. In the interests of team-strengthening most employed one or two professionals and by 1849, when the first Holkham cricket week was held, the Earl of Leicester, no mean cricketer himself, had engaged James Grundy, a noted all-rounder from Nottingham. Holkham were then entertaining teams like I. Zingari and M.C.C.

The Colman Brothers

A SCORE-BOOK page recording one of several matches in 1845-6, which featured the unique XI of Colman Brothers. Although the game shown against Letheringsett and Holt was drawn, the Brothers had defeated that team on previous occasions. The Brothers also played Norwich twice, losing by six wickets in one match and drawing a tight unfinished game in the other.

A fine cricket field had been laid out at Lakenham in 1827 by Henry Bentley from Lord's, but it was later that Jeremiah James Colman, an avid cricket enthusiast, decided that Lakenham Cricket Ground should be set aside for the "noble game" and other sports. County cricket resumed there in 1879 and the first Norwich Cricket Week was staged in 1881.

The Great Cricket Match at Sandringham

WHAT was headlined as "The Great Cricket Match at Sandringham" between I. Zingari and Gentlemen of Norfolk took place in mid-July 1866. The game had been keenly awaited by "the lovers of good cricket", particularly because the Prince of Wales was included in the I. Zingari team.

Both days of the match were blessed with fine weather and the Princess of Wales, Prince Albert Victor, the Mayor of Lynn and a host of local gentry were in attendance. Tents had been erected in which the players and their guests enjoyed sumptuous luncheons, but "simple" folk such as the estate tenants were present as well. The

I. Zingari - The Prince of Wales is sitting on the chair in the middle and Princess Alexandra on the chair on the right. Between them is Lord Suffield

Gentlemen of Norfolk - Charles Wright is sitting on the chair on the right

game was played out in truly beautiful surroundings and a band entertained in the interval.

The Gentlemen of Norfolk could total only 119 runs in their first innings and then, when I. Zingari went in, the Prince of Wales opened. But, perhaps to the disappointment of the spectators, he was bowled for a duck by Charles Wright, a Dereham solicitor formerly of Litcham. Employing a fast round-arm action Wright had been the County's top bowler for many years. In spite of the Prince's duck, excellent batting saw I. Zingari reach 277, with R. A. Fitzgerald making 101. Norfolk went in again and could only muster another 60 runs, leaving I. Zingari the victors by an innings and 98. Captain Henry Arkwright, a well-known player of the day, took fifteen of the Norfolk wickets. However, the cameo innings of 15 in Norfolk's second knock by W. Vyse, a Litcham player, included one "6" and one "5".

In 1935 the Norfolk County Cricket Club scorebook, in which the match details were recorded, came to light in a cupboard in St. James's Palace. The then Prince of Wales presented the book to the County Cricket Club and it now resides in the Norfolk Record Office.

ABORIGINAL AUSTRALIANS *v.* CARROW.

THIS CRICKET MATCH

WILL TAKE PLACE ON THE

OLD LAKENHAM CRICKET GROUND, NORWICH,

On THURSDAY and FRIDAY, the 23rd and 24th JULY inst.

Several well-known Cricketers will contend against the Blacks.

THE CARROW BAND WILL ATTEND EACH DAY.

ON FRIDAY,

At the Conclusion of the Match, there will be AUSTRALIAN and ENGLISH SPORTS, in
which the BLACKS will COMPETE.

BLACKS WITH BOOMERANGS
BLACKS WITH SPEARS.
LAURENCE'S FEAT WITH BAT AND BALL
DICK A DICK DODGING THE CRICKET BALL!!!!

ADMISSION, ONE SHILLING EACH.   CHILDREN HALF-PRICE.

Wickets to be pitched at Eleven o'clock each day.   (5820

THE Australian Aboriginals, the first overseas tourists to England, created a sensation in 1868, no more so than in Norwich where they met Carrow before a big crowd at Lakenham. The scorecard shows that the Aboriginals were allotted colours, presumably to help spectators with identification!

Having suffered some heavy reverses against professional sides, the tourists showed "a wonderful im-provement" and "whether in the field or at the wicket (they) exhibited a degree of activity and practised skill that was overwhelming". Against Carrow the bowling of Lawrence, the captain who had turned out for Surrey, and Mullagh was "formidable in the extreme" and the visitors won by an innings and 52 runs. On the tour both Mullagh and Cuzens achieved the double of 1,000 runs and 100 wickets.

At the conclusion of the match on the second day, the Aboriginals delighted an ever-growing crowd by competing in (and winning) foot races, then giving demonstrations of spear and boomerang throwing. The local press commented that they were "decidedly an attraction worthy of commendation".

THE AUSTRALIAN ELEVEN v. CARROW CLUB,

On Thursday & Friday, July 23 & 24, 1868,

ON THE LAKENHAM CRICKET GROUND.

CARROW CLUB.	First Innings.	Second Innings.
Humphrey W.	b Lawrence ... 26	c Mullagh, b Lawrence 16
Dix William	c Mullagh, b Lawrence 10	b Lawrence ... 6
Colman F. E.	b Mullagh ... 15	not out ... 8
Mitchell H.	b Lawrence ... 0	b Red Cap ... 2
Vyse W.	b Mullagh ... 9	l.b.w, b Lawrence ... 16
Colman B.	run out ... 12	b Lawrence ... 1
D'Eye P. C. R.	b Mullagh ... 0	c Red Cap, b Lawrence 11
Willett Ernest H.	b Lawrence ... 0	b Lawrence ... 6
Colman Arthur	run out ... 2	b Dick-a-Dick ... 17
Barwell H. G.	b Mullagh ... 1	c Dk-a-Dk b Lawrence 5
Dix Thomas	not out ... 0	b Lawrence ... 11
	b 3, l-b 2, w 2 ... 7	b 1, l-b 1, w 0 ... 2
	Total ... 82	Total ... 101

THE AUSTRALIANS		
Bullocky ...(Chocolate) run out ... 21		
Mullagh ...(Dark Blue) c and b Humphrey ... 42		
Cuzens ...(White) c F.E Colman, b Willett 87		
Twopenny ...(Drab) b E. Willett ... 17		
Tiger ...(Pink) b E. Willett ... 0		
Lawrence ...(Captain) c F.E.Colman b Willett 20		
Red Cap ...(Black) run out ... 20		
Dick-a-Dick ...(Yellow) c T. Dix, b W. Dix ... 5		
C. Dumas ...(Brown) b E. Willett ... 0		
Jim Crow (Light Blue) b. W. Dix ... 1		
Mosquito ...(Magenta) not out ... 1		
b 11, l-b 2, w 8 ... 21		
Total ... 235	Total ...

Umpires—Shephard and Henry Colman.

Norfolk Prospers

THE Norfolk team, which defeated Leicestershire by an innings and 48 runs in 1883. The imposing figure with blazer and cap in the back row is Henry Birkbeck, an excellent bat, while sitting in front of him is Rev. A. P. Wickham, a legendary wicket-keeper who later played for Somerset. Second from left in the back

row is Charles Jarvis and first left in the middle row is Lewis "Kerry" Jarvis. These brothers gave Norfolk sterling service in the 1880s.

Although boasting seven professionals, Leicestershire were dismissed for 43 and 88, thanks largely to schoolmaster Philip Morton, a fast bowler, who returned match figures of 12-40.

Lewis K. Kerry" Jarvis, Norfolk County Cricket Club's most successful batsman of the 1880s, (pictured second from right in the back row) in his Cambridge University days. He won a blue in the years 1877-1879 inclusive and was a member of the famous University side which defeated the Australians in 1878.

Born at Middleton Towers, the family home near King's Lynn, Jarvis invariably opened the Norfolk innings and topped the batting averages in several seasons. Against M.C.C. in 1883 he hit 103 at Lord's and 131 at Norwich. Perhaps his finest performance was in 1882 when, facing Bedfordshire's deadly accurate bowling, he carried his bat for 75 not out in a total of 130 in the first innings and then scored 50 out of 109 in the second.

Alexander, Frederick and Charles, his brothers, also served the County club, much the most successful of these being Charles, who captained Harrow to victory over Eton at Lord's in 1878.

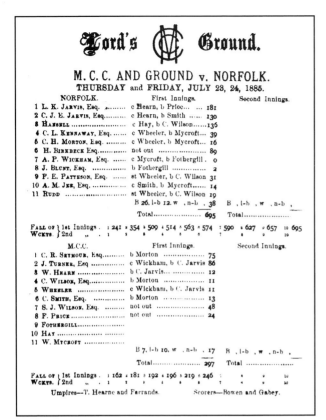

Lord's M.C.C. Ground.

M.C.C. AND GROUND v. NORFOLK.
THURSDAY and FRIDAY, JULY 23, 24, 1885.

NORFOLK.	First Innings.		Second Innings.
1 L. K. JARVIS, Esq.	c Hearn, b Price	181	
2 C. J. E. JARVIS, Esq.	c Hearn, b Smith	130	
8 HANSELL	c Hay, b C. Wilson	136	
4 C. L. KENNAWAY, Esq.	c Wheeler, b Mycroft	39	
6 C. H. MORTON, Esq.	c Wheeler, b Mycroft	16	
6 H. BIRKBECK Esq.	not out	89	
7 A. P. WICKHAM, Esq.	c Mycroft, b Fothergill	0	
8 J. BLUNT, Esq.	b Fothergill	2	
9 F. E. PATTESON, Esq.	st Wheeler, b C. Wilson	31	
10 A. M. JEE, Esq.	c Smith, b Mycroft	14	
11 RUDD	st Wheeler, b C. Wilson	19	
	B 26, l-b 12. w , n-b ,	38	B , l-b , w , n-b ,
	Total	695	Total

FALL OF 1st Innings . 1 241 2 354 3 509 4 514 5 563 6 574 7 590 8 627 9 657 10 695
WCKTS. 2nd   „ . 1   2   3   4   5   6   7   8   9   10

M.C.C.	First Innings.		Second Innings.
1 C. R. SEYMOUR, Esq.	b Morton	75	
2 J. TURNER, Esq	c Wickham, b C. Jarvis	86	
8 W. HEARN	b C. Jarvis	12	
4 C. WILSON, Esq.	b Morton	11	
6 WHEELER	c Wickham, b C. Jarvis	11	
6 C. SMITH, Esq.	b Morton	13	
7 S. J. WILSON, Esq.	not out	48	
8 F. PRICE	not out	24	
9 FOTHERGILL			
10 HAY			
11 W. MYCROFT			
	B 7, l-b 10, w , n-b ,	17	B , l-b , w , n-b ,
	Total	297	Total

FALL OF 1st Innings . 1 162 2 181 3 192 4 196 5 219 6 246 7   8   9   10
WCKTS. 2nd   „ . 1   2   3   4   5   6   7   8   9   10

Umpires—T. Hearne and Farrands.   Scorers—Bowen and Gabey.

Norfolk's total of 695, shown on this scorecard of a famous match, was at the time, and for some time after, the highest total made at Lord's. The first wicket partnership between the Jarvis brothers realised 241 runs.

However, two years later at Southampton, Francis E. Lacey, later to become Secretary of the M.C.C., made 323 not out for Hampshire against Norfolk - still a record for an individual score in a Minor Counties game. The bat, with which Lacey thrashed the Norfolk attack, resides in the M.C.C. collection at Lord's.

Clubs of the Day

THICKTHORN Hall Cricket Club in the late 1870s, when it was one of the many clubs associated with big houses. Frederick Watson, a solicitor, lived at the Hall and his sons George William and Herbert are third and fourth from the left in the back row. John, another son, is sitting in front of Herbert. Among other team members were probably sons of the staff of the houses.

Neighbouring teams

included Hethersett and Hethersett Reading Room, for both of which members of the Watson family turned out on occasions.

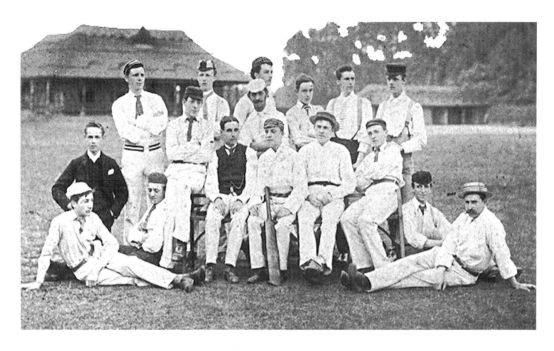

South Heigham Cricket Club in 1887, pictured (above) at Lakenham, its home ground. The young man on the left in a dark suit is Edwin Saul, who may have arrived too late to change for the photo-call!

Founded in 1883, South Heigham soon became one of Norwich's leading clubs and in 1886 was listed as having 40 members. In 1891 the club reached the semi-finals of the Senior Cup, only to lose to Yarmouth by 45 runs. Soon after it seems to have folded.

A match (lower left) at Garboldisham's ground, "The Langley", in the 1890s. The wicket-keeper is thought to be Rev. Charles Kennaway, the bowler Jesse Barnes and the umpire at the bowler's end Edgar Crowe of Ling Farm. Barnes and Arthur Read, the gardener at Garboldisham Manor, were the two professionals of the Manor's team. The Manor entertained the likes of I. Zingari and the Free Foresters, K. L. Gibson making 114 against the former in 1909.

From the mid-19th century the land-owning Montgomerie family had fostered the sport in the village and cricket weeks were popular. Norfolk entertained I. Zingari there several times and, from 1860 to the 1890s, Suffolk Borderers, captained for a time by Rev. Kennaway, were based at Garboldisham.

Rev. Kennaway, Vicar of the Parish 1876-1914, was a sound batsman who played for Norfolk many times, his highest score for the County being 147 against the Free Foresters in 1882.

Ladies' matches were popular at Narborough Hall Park in the early 1890s. Mr. Joseph Critchley Martin lived at the Hall and it was almost certainly Constance, his wife, who encouraged the game among the fairer sex. The picture (above) was taken on 23rd July 1890 during a match between teams billed as "Norfolk Foxhounds" and "Suffolk Harriers". Mr. Martin is sitting in the centre of the group and Constance is on a chair at his right hand.

Women's participation was nothing new, for in 1823 at Hockwold-cum-Wilton, 11 married females had defeated 11 single females for a prize of 11 pairs of gloves. Around the turn of the century, beautiful country-house grounds, like that at Narborough, were ideal settings in which ladies could enjoy the game; and in 1909 at Morley Hall, near Wymondham, Miss Jacob's Morley XI defeated Miss Upcher's Hingham XI by 24 runs. In the 1920s Rosalind, daughter of Sir Edward Stracey of Rackheath Hall, often turned out for the village's second XI. Indeed, just before the last War, womens' matches were popular with teams such as Aylsham, Dereham Jentique and Sennowe Park. There was also a County ladies' side.

The Wymondham Grammar School team, which won the Norwich Shield for Schools in 1891, the first year of the competition. In the final at Lakenham the Wymondham boys defeated the Paston Grammar School by nine wickets.

Unfortunately the Shield was not ready in time for presentation at the final. However, on returning to Wymondham, the victors were drawn from the Railway Station in a waggonette, "the band marching in front playing a lively tune".

EVEN modest clubs like Upper Sheringham produced quite decorative fixture cards.

In 1893 Upper Sheringham were dismissed for a paltry five runs in the first innings by Field Dalling, both Hammond and Massingham performing the hat trick. However, in the same season, Holt Grammar School could only muster a wretched three runs against Fulmodestone!

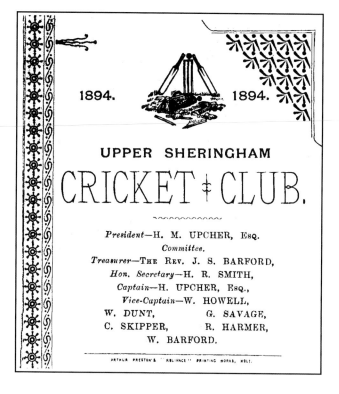

1894.   1894.

UPPER SHERINGHAM

CRICKET ‡ CLUB.

President—H. M. UPCHER, Esq.
Committee.
Treasurer—THE REV. J. S. BARFORD,
Hon. Secretary—H. R. SMITH,
Captain—H. UPCHER, Esq.,
Vice-Captain—W. HOWELL,
W. DUNT,   G. SAVAGE,
C. SKIPPER,   R. HARMER,
W. BARFORD.

ARTHUR PRESTON'S "RELIANCE" PRINTING WORKS, HOLT.

East Dereham's records for 1891 show the club was competing against some top local teams - among them Billingford Incapables and Ryburgh Invincibles! The first three in the batting averages that year had all represented the County.

There is evidence of an East Dereham side entertaining Shipdham as far back as 1788. However, the present club claims its existence from a meeting in the town's King's Head Inn in 1856, though refoundation took place in 1884. Earlier County matches had been played at Dereham.

The Norfolk and Norwich fixture card for 1886 - the year the club won the Norfolk Challenge Cup (later the Senior Cup). The competition had been instituted in 1884. After defeating Melton Constable in the final, the team celebrated at its annual dinner in the City's Bell Hotel. Scratching from the 1888 competition, the club folded some years later.

The Carrow team which defeated Dereham 218-85 in the final of the Senior Cup in 1889. Holding the trophy is R. J. Colman, though the captain of the side was Ferneley Cozens-Hardy (seated third from left). Archie, another member of the Cozens-Hardy family, is second from left in the back row.

The outstanding batsman of the final was W. A. Thurgar, a County player, who scored 88 not out. He is third from the left in the back row, while another County stalwart, George Rye, a fine all-rounder, is seated on the extreme right.

Formerly known as Stoke (Holy Cross) C.C., the club was renamed Carrow from 1862 when Messrs. J. & J. Colman's famous milling and mustard works were moved to Norwich.

A bill advertising fixtures to be played on the new Recreation Ground at Great Yarmouth, which was opened in 1889. At the time there were eight teams based in the town.

Although there had been an earlier Yarmouth side when cricket was played on the Denes, Great Yarmouth C.C. was founded in 1889. The club soon made its mark, winning the Senior Cup in 1890 and 1891, defeating on both occasions Carrow, the former holders.

Chapter Two

The Golden Years

Norfolk's Rev. George Barkley Raikes epitomised the cricketing cleric in the Golden Age. He was good enough to be featured in "Famous cricketers and cricket grounds", edited by Charles Alcock and published by the News of the World in 1895

The Age of Elegance

THE Golden Age of cricket can be regarded as the period from about 1895 to the outbreak of the Great War in 1914. During that time cricket at all levels enjoyed immense popularity and the game was full of wonderful personalities. Stylish amateurs like C. B. Fry and K. S. Ranjitsinhji batted with gay abandon; and, of course, there was the legendary Dr. W. G. Grace.

Edward Gurney Buxton's tea party at Lakenham in July 1902 when I. Zingari beat Norfolk by seven wickets. Mr. Buxton was the County Secretary, while Redmond Buxton scored 111 for the winners

The elegant Edwardians flocked to watch their idols and cricket matches were great social occasions. Grace completed 1000 runs in May and reached his hundredth hundred in 1895. In that year too the Minor Counties Championship was introduced and Norfolk finished joint winners with Durham and Worcestershire.

Raikes - A Great Sporting Parson

BORN at Carleton Forehoe in 1873, the Rev. George Barkley Raikes made his debut for Norfolk in 1890 while still at Shrewsbury School.

He went on to Oxford University, where he won a blue in 1894 and 1895. At this time his club cricket was limited, though he did score a century for Wymondham against Norwich Union in 1893 and appeared for Thorpe in the 1894 Senior Cup Final. But he continued to turn out for Norfolk, topping the batting averages in 1893 and 1897.

Starting out as a medium fast bowler but later changing to leg breaks, he built up a reputation as a fine all-rounder. But his sporting prowess was not confined to cricket and he was a brilliant goalkeeper on the football field. He won his Norfolk County Colours for soccer whilst playing for Wymondham Town in the 1892-93 season and was a blue at Oxford. He kept goal for the legendary Corinthians and appeared in four full internationals for England.

He became curate of Portsea in Hampshire from 1897 to 1903 and did not appear for Norfolk during that period. However, from 1900 to 1902 he played nine matches for Hampshire, finishing second in that county's batting averages on 43.33 in the first year. The highlight was probably a splendid 77 against Yorkshire at Portsmouth when facing the bowling

Playing for Portsea Clergy against Sherborne School, Rev. G. B. Raikes made 185 out of 219. Sherborne were all out for 211

of Schofield Haigh and George Hirst. Though he held the post of Chaplain to the Duke of Portland between 1905 and 1920, he managed to play for Norfolk from 1904 to 1913. He topped the County's batting averages in 1904 and 1905, captaining the side in the latter year when they secured the Minor Counties Championship. But his greatest season was in 1910 when he was again captain and led the team once more to the Championship. In that year he headed both the batting and bowling averages, scoring 679 runs at 61.73 and taking 57 wickets at 10.67 apiece. He scored three centuries, two of which were made against Nottinghamshire II, and performed the hat trick against Suffolk.

Raikes played his final first-class game in August 1912 when he joined Michael Falcon in an England XI, which played a drawn game with the Australian tourists at Lakenham. His last appearance for Norfolk was against Staffordshire in 1913, a year when the Championship was again won. In 16 seasons for the County he scored 3415 runs at an average of 31.62, his top score being 145 against Suffolk in 1904. His 267 wickets for Norfolk cost just over 16 each. His appointment to the living of Bergh Apton in 1920 gave the local side a big boost. One of many telling performances was in May 1922 when he took 9-19, including a hat trick, against Woodton, then top-scored with 25. This village cricket was a far cry from the days when he played with the "greats" like C. B. Fry on the Parks at Oxford, but by now he was approaching his fiftieth birthday.

G. B. Raikes, the footballer, in England jersey and sporting a Corinthians cap

Some Other Norfolk Idols

TYPICAL of the hard-working professionals of his era, Charles Shore, who had appeared for Lancashire and Nottinghamshire, gave Norfolk excellent service between 1889 and 1901. As a wily slow left-arm spin bowler, he bagged 585 wickets in all matches for the County at an average of 13.11. Undoubtedly the highlight occurred at Lakenham in 1897 when he took all ten Durham wickets for 50 runs in the first innings, then followed with 6-22 in the second. Fast bowler Tom Morley, his contemporary, who had also played for Nottinghamshire, took 246 wickets for Norfolk at 15.67.

Charles Shore in April 1898

Philip Algernon Fryer stands beside the scoreboard recording his 306 for Wellingborough Masters against E. Scriven's XI on Northamptonshire's County Ground in 1898. Born of a prominent Wymondham family, he was educated at Wellingborough Grammar School, where he later became headmaster and a governor. He regularly appeared for Norfolk between 1890 and 1905, topping the batting averages in 1895 when he scored the County's only century that season - 129 against Oxfordshire. In 1908 he played a couple of useful games for Northamptonshire. An outstanding soccer player, he was one of four brothers in the Wymondham team which won the Norfolk Senior Cup in 1889; and he also played for Cambridge University and the Corinthians.

The talented all-rounder Albert Relf (opposite) came to Norfolk when Lord Grey de Wilton offered him a four year professional engagement at Houghton Hall. This enabled him to play for the County in 1898 and 1899 and he had a batting average of 34.24 with three centuries. An off break bowler of medium pace, he took 65 wickets at 18.85. After two seasons, he left Norfolk for an outstanding career with Sussex, which led to 13 Test appearances.

Grace at Lakenham

SEVERAL of the great cricketers of the day visited Lakenham, among them Henry Foster (Worcestershire) and the Australian Albert Trott, who had match figures of 12-80 for M.C.C. against Norfolk in 1897. The graceful Ranjitsinhji played four innings for Cambridgeshire at Norwich, the best of which was a mere 50. But it was in 1903 when Dr W. G. Grace made his first visit to the City that local cricket enthusiasts were really excited. Grace, probably the best known Englishman of his time, came down with London County, the club he had joined on leaving Gloucestershire in 1899.

Above: Albert Relf

Right: London County coming out to field at Lakenham on 3rd August 1903. Just in front of the bearded Grace is Charles Robson, the wicket-keeper and former Hampshire captain

Left: Grace stayed overnight with the Buxton family at Catton Hall in 1903. The young Desmond Buxton sits between Robson and Grace with Edward Gurney Buxton behind. Both Buxtons served the County Club as Secretary and President. Seated on the left is C. J. Posthuma, the great Dutch bowler who was playing for London County

Right: Pictured at Lakenham on 4th August 1903 Grace is flanked by Edward G. Buxton (left) and Charles Robson

Below: London County's Charles Robson and Kenneth Barker pose at Lakenham in August 1903. Barker, a former player for Surrey and Cambridge University, took 11 Norfolk wickets in the match

Right: Grace returning to the pavilion on 4th August 1903 after being bowled by Worman for 31 in the second innings

On the opening day, Norfolk totalled 138 in their first innings and there was great expectancy from almost 3000 spectators as the Doctor went out to open the innings for the visitors. Sensationally, "W.G.", who was then aged 55 but still a feared batsman, played the fourth ball he received from James Worman on to his stumps and was out for a duck

London County were dismissed for 67 and Norfolk went in again and made 74. Grace top-scored with 31 in London County's second knock, but was again cleaned bowled by Worman. The innings closed at 83 and Norfolk had won by 62 runs.

Worman, a King's Lynn Grammar School master, had arrived in Norfolk from Midhurst in Sussex in 1894. That year, he scored four centuries for the school and initially made a big impression with his batting. Later, his principal role was that of a medium pace off break bowler and in his Norfolk County career between 1897 and 1908 he took 166 wickets at 15.71 each. Then he moved to Lincolnshire.

In 1904, Grace again visited Lakenham with London County, who were this time strengthened by the inclusion of William Murdoch, the former Sussex and Australian captain. But once more Norfolk were victorious, on this occasion by 139 and 236 (Rev. G. B. Raikes 74) to 194 and 97. Failing again, Grace was "caught Gibson bowled G. B. Raikes 17" in the first innings and "bowled (middle stump) Smith 6" in the second. In that second innings, William Smith, who gave great service to Norfolk as an off break bowler, took 9-28 which earned him a collection of £8.15s (£8.75) from appreciative spectators around the ground.

In the following match at Lakenham that Summer, a twenty-one year old batsman playing for Cambridgeshire did rather better than Grace had done. The youngster hit 92 and his name was John Berry Hobbs, later to find immortality with Surrey and England.

Grace with the great Australian batsman and captain Billy Murdoch at Lakenham in 1904

County Matters

The Norfolk team on August Bank Holiday Monday, 1908, during their drawn encounter with Hertfordshire. Back row, left to right: T. H. Wharton, Geo. Stevens, G. A. Stevens, M. Falcon; middle row: H. C. Dunell, B. Cozens-Hardy, L. Barratt, J. N. Worman, A. K. Watson; Front row: C. Dunning, E. Gibson. Geoffrey Stevens scored 118 not out in the second innings

THE visits of Grace were not the only highlights at Lakenham in the period before the Great War. In 1900 and again in 1906, Norfolk entertained the emerging West Indians, but each time the County lost by an innings. On the first occasion Shore took 5-64, whilst on the second Basil Cozens-Hardy made a creditable 48. It was in the later match that Michael Falcon, a Harrow schoolboy, made his Norfolk debut. By 1914, this outstanding all-rounder had gained four Cambridge blues, shone for the Gentlemen against the Players and taken over the Norfolk captaincy.

Norfolk leave the field in a match at Lakenham c.1910

28

In 1906 Geoffrey Stevens too made his County debut in a match against the Free Foresters - and his remarkable record speaks for itself. In 19 Minor Counties seasons he amassed 8333 Championship runs at 32.93, including 13 centuries and two double centuries. He scored a magnificent 201 to help Norfolk win the 1910 Challenge Match and captained the County in some matches when they again won the Championship in 1913.

Five Norfolk County professionals pictured about 1910. Back row, left to right: Ted Gibson, George Rye, Tommy Allsopp; front: Roderick Falconer and Harold Watson. Rye had finished playing for the County in 1895 but stood as a Minor Counties umpire from 1896 to 1932

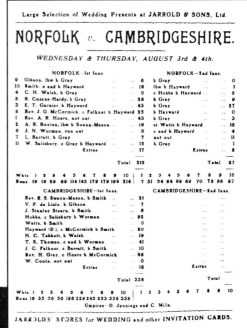

NORFOLK v. CAMBRIDGESHIRE.

WEDNESDAY & THURSDAY, AUGUST 3rd & 4th.

NORFOLK—1st Inns.		NORFOLK—2nd Inns.	
9 Gibson, lbw b Gray	6	b Gray	0
10 Smith, c and b Hayward	16	lbw b Hayward	1
4 C. H. Walsh, b Gray	0	c Hobbs b Hayward	5
5 B. Cozens-Hardy, b Gray	26	b Gray	9
3 E. T. Garnier, b Hayward	43	b Gray	27
6 Rev. J. G. McCormick, c Falkner b Hayward	25	b Hayward	0
1 Rev. A. R. Hoare, not out	43	b Gray	5
2 A. R. Buxton, lbw b Swann-Mason	19	st Watts b Hayward	18
8 J. N. Worman, run out	0	c and b Hayward	4
7 L. Barratt, b Gray	7	not out	11
11 W. Salisbury, c Gray b Hayward	12	b Gray	0
Extras	17	Extras	8
Total	**215**	**Total**	**87**

Wkts.	1	2	3	4	5	6	7	8	9	10	1	2	3	4	5	6	7	8	9	10
Runs	19	19	29	69	114	145	179	179	199	214	7	51	54	64	69	69	70	75	86	87

CAMBRIDGESHIRE—1st Inns.		CAMBRIDGESHIRE—2nd Inns.	
Rev. R. S. Swann-Mason, b Smith	31	...	
V. F. de Lisle, b Gibson	7	...	
J. Stanley Stearn, b Smith	6	...	
Hobbs, c Salisbury b Worman	92	...	
Watts, b Smith	0	...	
Hayward (D.), c McCormick b Smith	80	...	
H. C. Tebbutt, b Walsh	19	...	
T. S. Thomas, c and b Worman	41	...	
J. C. Falkner, c Barratt b Smith	10	...	
Rev. H. Gray, c Hoare b McCormick	36	...	
W. Coote, not out	0	...	
Extras	16	Extras	...
Total	**338**	**Total**	

Wkts.	1	2	3	4	5	6	7	8	9	10	1	2	3	4	5	6	7	8	9	10
Runs	16	35	56	56	198	229	242	253	338	338										

Umpires—D. Jennings and C. Mills.

In these successes Norfolk was also well served by paid players - Tommy Allsopp, Ted Gibson, Harold Watson, Roderick Falconer and the Lynn professional George Stevens. Allsopp, a Norwich City footballer, was a useful all-rounder, while Gibson, a slow bowler, bagged 425 wickets at 16.92 between 1902 and 1914. In the three seasons leading to the War, Falconer, a former Northamptonshire medium pace bowler, captured 129 wickets at 11.53.

Harold Watson, a medium to fast bowler, was on the Lord's ground staff when he captured the wicket of the mighty Frank Woolley with his first ball in first-class cricket. For Norfolk, between 1910 and 1927, he took 384 wickets at just over 18 apiece.

In an age when there was still much strict class distinction and the game was run by amateurs, the professional's life was not easy, but he did enjoy regular pay and possibly a benefit. The redoubtable George Rye, who bagged 264 wickets for Norfolk in the 18 seasons leading up to 1895, received a benefit of about £50 in 1894. Much later in 1922, Watson's contract with Norfolk guaranteed him £5 a week in the Summer and £1 a week in the Winter, plus match expenses. "Talent money" was available in the form of £1 for every 50 runs scored and seven wickets taken in an innings. But after the War, the old order declined and the professional's lot improved.

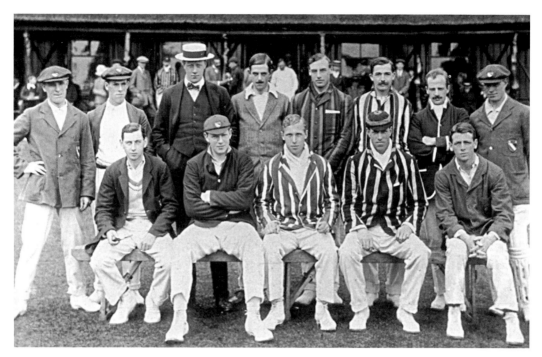

Norfolk C.C. in 1912. Back row, left to right: E. Gibson, H. Watson, C. B. L. Prior (Hon. Sec.), R. W. Thurgar, R. F. Popham, G. W. Birkbeck, L. F. Wynne-Willson, R. Falconer; Front Row: E. J. Fulcher, G. A. Stevens, M. Falcon (capt.), Rev. G. B. Raikes, R. G. Pilch

Play Up School!

THERE was no Eton or Harrow in Norfolk, but school cricket flourished. Often the masters had been coached at University and perhaps the boys wanted to emulate their heroes in "The Boy's Own Paper" and other juvenile periodicals. In 1891, three shields were presented by Mr. S. Gurney Buxton for competition by "Public Elementary and other Schools" in the Lynn, Norwich and Yarmouth Districts. Among the better teams were those representing the grammar schools at Gresham, King's Lynn, Norwich, North Walsham (Paston), Thetford, Wymondham and Yarmouth.

Cromer's Suffield Park School playing a match during one of those balmy Summer days in the Edwardian era when Mr H. Gordon Winter was the Headmaster. The School was a preparatory school for the Public Schools and Norfolk's great Michael Falcon captained the School XI before going up to Harrow.

Cricket was encouraged in many public elementary schools and this charming picture is of the village school team at Weasenham All Saints about 1910. The mistress is Mrs Ann "Jotty" Smith.

The Thetford Grammar School First XI stand proudly on the steps of their pavilion in 1911. In the middle row are E. P. Hogg (second from the left) and George Neville (fourth from the left), who both went on to make their mark in local cricket. Neville, like fellow Old Thetfordians Reggie Cant and Harold Watson, played for Norfolk. In 1913, Thetford Grammar School became the only school ever to win the Norfolk Junior Cup. Sadly the pavilion was burnt down in 1980.

In 1909, St James's Council School for boys, built on London Road at King's Lynn in 1893, was the first winner of the new magnificent Lynn & District Schools Shield. Once the face of the original shield had been covered in names, the rules provided for it to be given to the school whose name appeared most times.

A Quick Run Round The Clubs

A TYPICAL country scene with cricket on the Green at Martham in 1907. The village team did not play on the Green after the First World War and moved to a private meadow. Local clubs were fervently supported and there was much rivalry between neighbouring villages. In 1892, Martham had reached the Junior Cup Final, only to lose heavily to Diss, for whom R. H. Mornement scored 132.

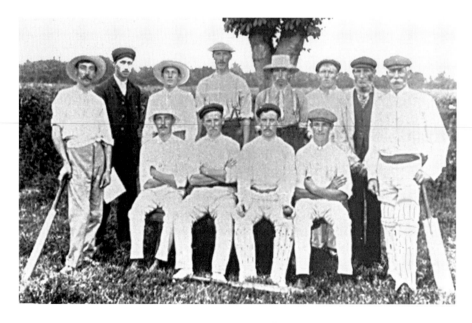

The Terrington St Clement team posing on their cricket field at Alma Lodge, then the home of Mrs. Frances Walker. Four of the team were from the Howling family and five of those pictured lost their lives in the First World War.

The church makes a delightful backdrop to this picture of the Kilverstone team. The cricket field was in front of the church and was part of the estate of the Fisher family, who lived at the Hall. No cattle were allowed on the field and the pitch, laid with Cumberland turf, was lovingly maintained by the Kilverstone Hall gardeners. The village raised a team until about 1960.

In this array of fixture cards, all the featured clubs existed before the Great War except Barleycorns. However, the renowned Norwich Wanderers did not play their first game until May 1913 when they beat Carrow 55-33, Eric Fulcher taking 5-8 and Harold Dougill 5-5. Dougill and Fulcher, like Geoffrey Stevens who was also in the side, were County players. In 1909, Stevens had helped C.E.Y.M.S. to victory over Norwich Teachers in the Senior Cup Final, one of the Church's other stars being R. G. Pilch.

In the lazy Summer holidays between 1903 and 1914, Basil Cozens-Hardy (seated third from the right in the middle row) ran this side called the Holiday Hittites. The team, whose headquarters was at the Old Schoolhouse ground in Holt, was made up of old County players, local gentry, parsons and visitors. Among their opponents were Cromer, Overstrand and Sidestrand. Jack Skrimshire, a popular Melton Constable doctor who had played for the County, and who is seated third from the left in the middle row, scored 200 not out for the Hittites against C.E.Y.M.S. in 1908.

Pictured in front of the grandstand at the Wellesley Road Recreation Ground in Great Yarmouth on 15th August 1905 are two teams of veterans. In the game, which was in aid of the Boy's Home, Mr. C. Brasnett's XI defeated Mr. C. Papworth's XI 157-96. For the winners, C. "Felix" Panchen, wearing pads in the front row, top-scored with 75. The match became an annual affair up to the Great War and proceeds always went to various local charities. In 1909, the age range was 65-83!

Country-House Cricket

WITH a wealth of big halls and titled families, it was not surprising that country-house cricket flourished in Norfolk. The amateur cricketers of the gentry enjoyed the sport on the beautiful grounds of halls like Didlington, Lexham, Hillington and, of course, Holkham and Houghton. During champagne-filled cricket weeks, house guests enjoyed lavish hospitality and partying in the evenings.

A family match on the lawn at Buckenham Tofts Hall in August 1909

A cricket lunch at Old Buckenham around 1912. Lionel Robinson is top of the table on the left, next to him Archie MacLaren followed by Charles Robson, formerly of Hampshire

Like Albert Relf at Houghton, many halls had at least one professional cricketer on the staff to strengthen their side. During cricket weeks other "pros" might play and, in 1897, F. R. Spofforth, "the Demon Bowler", and J. T. Hearne appeared at Houghton where "some brilliant cricket was displayed". In 1899 the local press deemed it sufficiently newsworthy to report that Morley, the Norfolk pro, was staying at Holkham Hall during its cricket week.

In 1887, shortly after taking up residence at his newly completed country seat, The Pleasaunce at Overstrand, Lord Battersea had a cricket pitch laid there. Just down the road, Sir Samuel Hoare did the same at Sidestrand Hall. Overstrand became a centre of excellent cricket and personalities like Ranjitsinhji and Henry Austin, an Eton College coach, appeared there.

Lionel Robinson, a flamboyant Australian financier, bought Old Buckenham Hall estate in 1906 and pulled the hall down to build himself a more modern residence. Wishing to take on the role of a country squire, he had a clearing made in a wood in the grounds so a cricket pitch could be laid. In the Winter of 1909 the whole meadow was returfed under the supervision of Alec Hearne, the old Kent player. In one corner of the ground a picturesque thatched pavilion was erected. Well-known players of the day appeared for Robinson's XI, which attracted first-class opposition. One cricketer who guested for Robinson's team was Archie MacLaren, the famous England batsman and captain.

Some of the South African tourists together with other well-known players line up with
Lionel Robinson at Old Buckenham in 1912

In 1912, Robinson appointed MacLaren as his private secretary and cricket manager, providing him with a house on the estate. In the same year, Robinson's XI, captained on this occasion by Bosanquet, the Middlesex and England amateur, defeated the South Africans by 191 runs.

Around that time playing for Old Buckenham village was Edward Groom, affectionately known as "Squibs", the name by which he was referred to when scores appeared in the local press. Although somewhat retarded, Squibs was a great-hearted little chap and a fine enthusiastic cricketer. In his autobiographical work "Spring Sowing", Michael Home, the Breckland author, recalls the first occasion Squibs played at a certain hall renowned for its cricket lunches served by butlers. On spying the fare, Squibs's eyes almost bulged out of their sockets. Talented village cricketers entered another world when they were good enough to be invited to play at the big houses!

Mr Alex Donovan lived at Carbrooke Hall, near Watton, and Home mentions an all-day game in which he played there against Donovan's XI. Gradually, through the day, players received telegrams and had to leave. In the end, the match was abandoned. It was August 1914 and Britain was at war. When the fighting ended, countless young cricketers would not return from the battlefields of the Continent to the cricket fields of England.

Chapter Three

Rip-Roaring Cricket in the Twenties

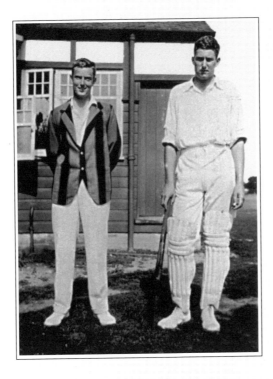

Basil Rought-Rought (left) and Rodney, his brother, who arrived on the Norfolk cricket scene in the mid-1920s. Together with their brother Desmond they made a big impact in the 1930s. Basil and Rodney made their debuts for South Norfolk C.C. in a match against Yarmouth Wanderers in 1925, whilst Desmond first appeared for the same team in 1929. All three went on to enjoy successful careers with the Norfolk County side.

The Legacy of Heath House to Norfolk

THE Heath House side, in which the Rought-Rought brothers began their cricketing careers, pictured in the early 1920s. Albert, their father (in the middle of the second row), ran a furrier's and hatter's business at Brandon; and Heath House was the work's team which he kitted out and arranged to be coached by Bill Hitch, the Surrey and England fast bowler.

In the picture the Rought-Rought brothers are:

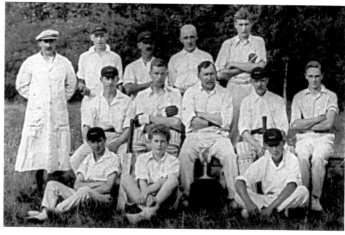

Basil W. (second from left in the middle row), a dependable left-handed opening bat who scored in all 4728 runs for Norfolk at an average of 22.51 between 1926 and 1948. In 1937 he headed the County batting averages in the Minor Counties' Championship with 757 runs at 50.46.

Rodney C. (extreme right in the back row), who took 462 wickets for the county at an average of 15.95 with his medium fast bowling. He also produced some useful scores lower down in the batting order and gained a Cambridge blue in 1930 and 1932. Early on in his Varsity career he took 7-36 against Middlesex.

Desmond (the middle boy on the grass) scored 3029 runs for Norfolk at an average of just over 25 and took 256 wickets at 21.37 apiece. He scored 92 against Sussex on his debut for Cambridge University, where he won a blue in 1937.

Also in the picture are Walter Eagle (second from left in the back row) and Percy Kent (bottom right sitting on the grass), who started with Heath House as ball boys. Eagle went on to play for Wisbech, but he had a few games for South Norfolk and enjoyed three good years (1930-1932) with the ball for Norfolk County Cricket Club. In 1924 Kent, a fast medium bowler who could swing a ball and turn it off the seam but was also a useful bat, received a two-year professional contract to play league cricket in Derbyshire. He later turned out for local sides like his native Weeting and Buckenham Tofts Hall.

Walter Bullock (sitting on the left on the grass) was a wicket-keeper batsman who moved to Norfolk in the late 1940s and gave many years service to Hempnall C.C., where at times he was groundsman, captain and later club president.

The "Test Match" at Old Buckenham

AFTER the Great War, Lionel Robinson and Archie MacLaren resumed the staging of top class country-house cricket matches on the beautiful ground at Old Buckenham Hall.

In 1921 they pulled off their biggest coup of all. Back in May 1919, Robinson's XII, captained then by J. R. Mason of Kent and including J. W. H. T. Douglas of Essex and the immortal Frank Woolley, had played a creditable draw with an Australian Imperial Forces' touring side packed with Test stars. However, it was the game in May 1921 that really caught the public's imagination when Robinson's XI met Warwick Armstrong's all-conquering

The Australian Team at Old Buckenham, 5th May 1921.
Standing, left to right: J. M. Taylor, J. M. Gregory, J. S. Ryder, H. L. Hendry, E. A. McDonald, W. Bardsley; Front, sitting: Mr. Smith (Manager), C. G. Macartney, W. W. Armstrong, Lionel Robinson, H. L. Collins; On ground: A. A. Mailey, H. Carter

Australians in the second match of their tour. Robinson's team, which MacLaren had assembled, boasted many of the day's top players, among them Chapman, Douglas, Fender, Hendren and the legendary Jack Hobbs.

On the first day of the historic match persistent rain allowed the bowling of only three overs, during which the Australians proceeded to 18 without loss.

By the following day the weather had improved and people flocked to Old Buckenham for "one of the most wonderful days in the history of Norfolk cricket". They arrived by pony and trap, horse and cart, motor cars, by bicycles and on foot. The roofs of some vehicles became temporary grandstands and the crowd was estimated at between 7000 and 10000 - the largest ever to watch a cricket game in Norfolk.

Despite Armstrong scoring 51 not out with some powerful drives and pulls, the mighty Australians were dismissed for a paltry 136, thanks largely to some fine seam bowling by John Douglas, who bowled unchanged, and Clement Gibson of Sussex.

Warwick Armstrong in full flow. Fender, Chapman and MacLaren are in the slips

Then Hobbs took the stage and, for the next hour and a half, he enthralled the crowd with the ease and elegance of his batting. Withstanding the fast hostile deliveries of Gregory and McDonald, he reached 85 before the recurrence of leg muscle trouble forced him to retire. Like Jupp, the Sussex amateur who damaged a thumb, he took no further part in the match.

Despite these setbacks, MacLaren was able to declare at 256 for 7 on the third day, but the weather again intervened and the game fizzled out to a draw. In their curtailed second innings the Australians had their backs to the wall and the accurate Gibson recorded the remarkable figures of 9-8-1-1.

Although the weather was disappointing, the local press commented: "To Norfolk the fixture has been a great and memorable event and the incidents of the match will be the gossip of the countryside and cricket pavilions for many years to come". And so it proved to be.

Years later, in July 1952, Jack Hobbs visited Lakenham to renew acquaintance with Bill

Top left: Armstrong and J. M. Taylor leave the field.

Above: Jack Hobbs and Donald Knight go out to open the innings for Robinson's XI.

Left: John White bowled by Gregory.

40

Fairservice, an old Kent player who at the time was scoring for Kent II. In the score-box keeping the records for Norfolk was Len Hart, a prominent figure in Norfolk cricket circles for several decades. In 1921 Hart was headmaster of Old Buckenham School and during the famous match he had accommodated Hobbs and Hendren. To Hart's delight, Hobbs recalled the game, saying that the 85 he made against Gregory and McDonald on that occasion was one of the finest innings of his career. He added, "They made me fight for every run."

The South Africans beaten

NORFOLK COUNTY CRICKET CLUB
NORWICH CRICKET WEEK,
AUGUST 6th to 11th, 1923.

NORFOLK V. HERTS.

NORFOLK — 1st Innings		NORFOLK — 2nd Innings	
1 M. Falcon c Driscoll b Thorley	51	not out	43
2 Nichols b Burton	0	lbw b Driscoll	19
3 G. R. R. Colman b Lismore	52	c Reid b Thorley	11
4 G. A. Stevens c. Grimsdell b Burton	87	st Grimsdell b Driscoll	36
5 Major J. Wormald b Lismore	0	b Burton	36
6 E. F. Long b Burton	51	c Hylton-Stewart b Reid	23
7 R. D. Carter b Hylton-Stewart	3		
8 T. B. Raikes c Grimsdell b Burton	7		
9 Watson c Lismore b Hylton-Stewart	13		
10 N. G. Evans lbw b Hylton-Stewart	0		
11 W. A. Beadsmoore not out	6		
Extras	21	Extras	2
Total	291	Total	170

Wkts.	1	2	3	4	5	6	7	8	9	10	1	2	3	4	5	6	7	8	9	10
Runs	2	70	123	125	243	243	253	274	274	291	49	85	87	122	170					

HERTS.—1st Innings		HERTS—2nd Innings	
1 C. B. G. Hunter b Watson	0		
2 A. Grimsdell b Falcon	48		
3 L. J. Reid c Nichols b Falcon	53		
4 C. H. Titchmarsh lbw b Long	3		
5 Lt. T. E. Halsey run out	0		
6 R. B. Cowley c Watson b Falcon	68		
7 J. J. Thorley c Watson b Long	24		
8 W. Lismore c Long b Watson	32		
9 B. D. Hylton-Stewart b Falcon	12		
10 Burton b Falcon	52		
11 R. Driscoll not out	4		
Extras	23	Extras	
Total	297	Total	

Wkts.	1	2	3	4	5	6	7	8	9	10	1	2	3	4	5	6	7	8	9	10
Runs	0	110	119	119,119	220	223	259	284	297											

THE Twenties was a decade of peaks and troughs for Norfolk County Cricket Club, the high point coming in 1922 when they headed the Minor Counties' table. Then, despite a fine knock of 98 by Geoffrey Colman in the first innings, the County lost the ensuing Challenge Match by eight runs to Buckinghamshire, who thus became Champions.

Several touring sides visited Lakenham and inflicted some heavy defeats on Norfolk. In 1923 it was the West Indies by 231 runs, in 1927 New Zealand by an innings and 97 runs and in 1929 the South Africans by an innings and 44 runs. In 1928 Norfolk trailed the West Indies by 26 runs on the first innings in a drawn encounter.

Above: Scorecard showing Edward Long's debut for Norfolk at the age of 46. The famous lob bowler only played one season for the county.

Right: Michael Falcon leads the Minor Counties XI out to field against the South Africans in 1924.

Undoubtedly, the outstanding game took place in 1924 when a Minor Counties' XI, albeit including seven Norfolk representatives, defeated the South Africans by 25 runs with only two minutes remaining. Included in the Minor Counties' team were Percy Chapman (Berkshire and later Kent) and R. J. O. Meyer, who later played for Somerset. Norfolk's Michael Falcon bagged three wickets in the tourists' first innings and five in the second.

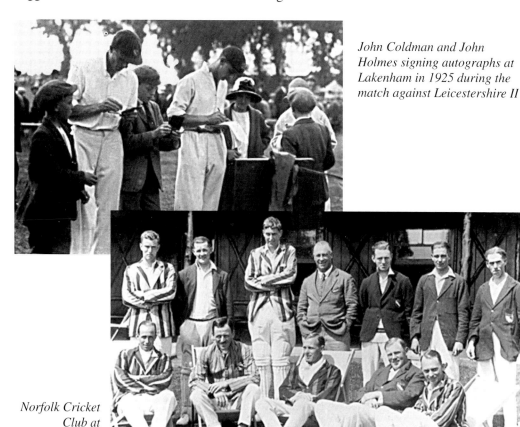

John Coldman and John Holmes signing autographs at Lakenham in 1925 during the match against Leicestershire II

Norfolk Cricket Club at Lakenham in 1927

Michael Falcon - A Norfolk Legend

MICHAEL Falcon gave incomparable service to Norfolk County Cricket Club. He played for the County between 1906 and 1946, topping the batting averages in his last season when he was then 58; and he captained the side from 1912 to 1946. In all matches for Norfolk, Falcon scored 12317 runs at an average of over 32 and took 743 wickets at 16.55. Later there were spells when he was Chairman and then President of the County Club.

It was in the 1920s that Falcon was at his most devastating. His career-best score of 205 was made against Hertfordshire at Cheshunt in 1920, while he enjoyed great success in 1922 when Norfolk lost that Minor Counties' Challenge Match to Buckinghamshire. That season he totalled 727 runs for the County at an average of 38.26 and took 60 wickets at 13.35 in Minor Counties' Championship games.

The great all-rounder could have pursued a first-class career, which would almost certainly have led to Test appearances, but he chose to stay loyal to his native county. Nevertheless, having won blues at Cambridge in the years 1908-11 inclusive, he made regular appearances for the Gentlemen against the Players between 1911 and 1926, distinguishing himself on many occasions. At the Oval in 1924 he took 7-78 in the Players' first innings and scored 34 not out in a last wicket stand of 134 with Arthur Gilligan. In 1926 he captained the M.C.C. against the Australians at Lord's and the same year took 7 for 42, playing for H. M. Martineau's XI against the tourists.

However, the highlight occurred at Eastbourne in late August 1921. Up to that point Armstrong's awesome Australians had been unbeaten on tour, but veteran Archie MacLaren got together a team, including Falcon, which he said could do the trick. And sure enough MacLaren's England XI scored a sensational victory by 28 runs, Falcon weighing in with figures of 6-67 in the tourist's first innings.

A. C. MacLaren's XI at Eastbourne, August 1921. Back row, left to right: H. Ashton, C. H. Gibson, A. P. F. Chapman, G. E. C. Wood, G. Ashton; Sitting: G. A. Faulkner, A. C. MacLaren (Captain), G. N. Foster, M. Falcon; Front: C. T. Ashton

Jack Hobbs in Norfolk

THE Norwich YMCA in St. Giles was fortunate to have the great Jack Hobbs (centre with bat) to open its nets in the mid-1920s. The nets were on the Bethel Street side of the building. Among Norfolk cricket personalities in the front row with Hobbs are R. G. Pilch (first left), Jack Read (fifth from left), John Holmes (fourth from right) and Harold Theobald (extreme right).

The South Norfolk Cricket Club

ALTHOUGH Lionel Robinson died in 1922, cricket continued to be played on his charming ground at Old Buckenham Hall and the South Norfolk Cricket Club, founded in 1923, made it their home. Ernest Gates, a Bradford industrialist, bought the hall from Robinson's widow, but he passed away in 1925. Everard, his son, then briefly brought back the great days of the Robinson era by staging some top class games there.

South Norfolk C.C. Tourists at Blackwell, Derbyshire, 1926

General Arrangements for Whitsuntide Tour, 1929.

N.B.—Members desirous of taking part in this Tour **must** inform the Secretary by May 1st.

Friday, May 17th.
Proceed to SKEGNESS via King's Lynn, Long Sutton, Fleet, Sutterton, Boston and Wainfleet. (100 miles from Norwich).
Members who require conveyance communicate with Secretary early.
Headquarters : - THE LUMLEY HOTEL, (opposite Station and Ground).

Saturday, May 18th.
South Norfolk v. Skegness
11-30 a.m.

Sunday, May 19th.
Members are asked to vacate their rooms by 10-0 a.m. as Leicester Amateurs are arriving at the Hotel.
GOLF has been arranged for at SUTTON-ON-SEA. (25 miles),—proceed thence via Alford– in evening on to LINCOLN via Louth and Wragby. (46 miles).
Alternative routes for non-Golfers
(a) via Boston (23) ; Sleaford (18) ; Lincoln (17) ; 58 miles.
(b) via Spilsby (12) ; Horncastle (10) ; Lincoln (21) ; 43 miles.
Headquarters : - - WHITE HART HOTEL.

Whit-Monday, May 20th.
South Norfolk v. Lincoln Lindum C.C.
11-30 a.m.
After match proceed to SLEAFORD (17 miles).
Headquarters : : : BRISTOL ARMS HOTEL.

Tuesday, May 21st.
Leave Sleaford 9-45 a m. for PETERBOROUGH (34 miles), via Bourne and Market Deeping.

South Norfolk v. Peterborough
11-30 a.m.
After match proceed to BOSTON (33 miles), via Crowland, Spalding, Gosberton and Sutterton.
Headquarters : WHITE HART HOTEL (by Bridge).

Wednesday, May 22nd.
Leave at 10-0 a.m. for SKEGNESS (23 miles).
South Norfolk v. Leicester Amateurs
11-30 a.m.
Return to Boston after Match. Same Headquarters.

Thursday, May 23rd.
Leave for SLEAFORD (18 miles), at 10-15 a m.
South Norfolk v. Sleaford
11-30 a.m.
After Match proceed to STAMFORD (29 miles).
Headquarters : - - - - GEORGE HOTEL.

Friday, May 24th.
Leave Stamford at 10-0 a.m. for KETTERING (22 miles).
South Norfolk v. Kettering
11-30 a.m.
Hotel arrangements to be made during week.

Umpire :
Mr. Leslie Barnard.

Scorer :
Mr. R. M. Palmer.

In 1926 an "Old Buckenham Hall Week" was held in the old style; and in one match Everard Gates's XI played H. D. Leveson-Gower's XI. Because of his mother's death, Leveson-Gower could not play, but his team was captained by Colin McIver, the Essex player. In the photograph of the occasion, McIver is padded up and fourth from

South Norfolk Whitsuntide Tour Programme 1929

the right in the front row with Gates next to him fifth from the right. On Gates's other side is Harry Simms, the old Sussex amateur.

The same year saw the South Norfolk Club acquire the professional services of Burnett Bullock, a former Surrey batsman, to coach and "to assist the cricket revival". However, Bullock, a spectacular hitter when he got going, only stayed a year, but nevertheless made a big impression.

From 1925 onwards for several years South Norfolk's cricketers enjoyed tours to Derbyshire, Leicestershire, Lincolnshire, Suffolk and Essex, and often their opponents included players with first-class experience. In the early years the party travelled around in the "Beer Bus" and the social side seemed as important as the cricket. Against Blackwell on the 1926 Derbyshire tour the team suffered a heavy reverse, despite Bullock scoring 51 out of a total of 78. Perhaps this can be attributed to the "red-letter night" before, when the party had wallowed in champagne to celebrate Gates's birthday. In the photograph of the touring party, Bullock is second from left in the front row, Gates is in the middle and Len Hart, the club secretary, is sixth from the left in the front and next to Gates. Hart recalled arriving home from this particular tour at 4 a.m. and then having to start an all-day game at Old Buckenham at 11 a.m.

E. E. Gates's XI and H. D. G. Leveson-Gower's XI at Old Buckenham, July 1926

During the close season, the South Norfolk Cricket Club held grand dances and lavish dinners at popular venues in Norwich, but in spite of the revelling there were some fine performances on the cricket field. Against the Gentlemen of Suffolk at Felixstowe in 1928, Dr. J. H. Owens (71) and Basil Rought-Rought (111) put on 204 for the first wicket towards a total of 426. The match was won by an innings and 173 runs.

When bowlers held the upper hand

ALTHOUGH looking ill-equipped for cricket, Wicklewood C.C., pictured on the next page in the late Twenties, seemed to have made an effort on their pitch. The club's accounts for 1927 record the purchase of a new mower for £1.15.9 (£1.79) and repair of the roller.

However, high scores were at a premium in village cricket, thanks largely to the length of the grass, particularly in the outfield, and the unpredictable wickets. Extraordinary bowling

figures were being returned every week and, in 1928, John Walwyn took 9-8 for Carleton Forehoe against Wicklewood in a Wicklewood and District League match.

Among many fine analyses recorded elsewhere was that of 9-9 by R. W. Laws for King's Lynn II against Grimston in 1921. In 1928 P. Rayner took 8-2 playing for Swanton Morley against Horningtoft in the Boyle Cup, whilst the same year saw T. Alderton have an incredible return of 6-0 for Great Cressingham against Saham Toney.

In an astonishing match in the Freethorpe and District League in 1927 Halvergate totalled only 18, but then they dismissed Reedham for four! E. Nicholls scored Reedham's four runs with his ten colleagues all making ducks!

With the odds stacked against the batsmen, "tons" were rarely recorded in village scorebooks, so W. Wyett's 104 not out for Wretham (175-5) versus Old Buckenham (112) in 1923 was most praiseworthy. But on the well-manicured estate pitches of the country houses the runs flowed more freely. George Neville, who led Feltwell to Junior Cup success in 1922, took a century off Australia House for Lionel Robinson's XI at Old Buckenham Hall the same year. The press commented: "Playing chiefly in village cricket where the outfield is a handicap to fast or big scores, this was his first century for five years." Neville, who went on to captain Wisbech and played a handful of games for the County, is seen third from right on the front row of the South Norfolk touring party on page 30.

Pictured second from left in the back row of this Mundford and Lynford team of the 1920s is Sidney George Causton. While turning out for nearby Didlington against Northwold on 15th May 1922, he performed the hat trick twice. Although taking seven wickets for 39 runs, he could not prevent Northwold from winning by 34 runs, thanks largely to W. R. Eng-lish's 41 not out.

Arthur and Herbert, Sidney's sons, were bagging wickets for Mundford in the Thirties; and amazingly Nick, his great grandson, took six wickets in six balls for Brooke in 1996. Nick's feat is referred to on page 93.

Fifth from the left in the back row of this Garboldisham team of the Twenties is Albert Beales, who produced a remarkable spell of bowling on 7th September 1922. Dismissed by Botesdale for 26 runs, Garboldisham must have thought they were heading for defeat, but Beales had other ideas. Bowling with a sharp swing from leg and a nip off the pitch, he took an incredible 10 wickets for one run and Garboldisham won by five runs. Nine of his victims were clean bowled and he took the last four wickets in five balls.

A press report commented there had been nothing wrong with the pitch, while Beales claimed "a wide awake slip" could have prevented the one run he conceded!

Coming from Quidenham to Garboldisham Manor as a gardener, he soon showed remarkable consistency, as these seasonal records show:

	Overs	Maidens	Runs	Wickets	Average
1922	306	77	546	130	4.2
1923	242	52	449	110	4.09
1924	449	101	867	180	4.14

Even in his last season, in 1949 when then aged 64, he bagged 30 wickets at an average of 7.00.

The man sitting on the right in the photograph is the Rev. Charles A. Sturges-Jones, and sitting next to him is Dr. J. H. Walton, one of the village side's principal batsmen. Seated in the middle is Sidney Whiting.

The grass was high on the field when this picture of Morley C.C. was taken in the 1920s. Sitting at the front are Vic Bell (left) and Reggie (Shorty) Long, a fine medium pace bowler who joined the club when it was founded in 1922 and went on to captain it from 1930 to the late 1950s.

Morley's finest hour came in 1929 when they beat the high-ranking Carrow team at Lakenham. A generous lady of the village decided that the team should have a set of caps for the big occasion and she purchased enough

Wolf Cub-style caps to equip them. She then arranged for other female supporters to sew on badges with the initials "M.C.C.". When the village side emerged from the Lakenham pavilion a Carrow spectator, who did not recognise them, asked the Morley captain from what school did they come!

"School", replied the captain, "They're nearly all clodhoppers". But even so, on that day, they defeated their more illustrious opponents.

A Social Occasion for Village and Club

ALTHOUGH not competing with the scrumptious fare in which cricketers indulged during all-day matches at the large country houses, cricket teas and socialising were enjoyed by village teams.

Heaps of sandwiches and a splendid urn adorn the table (below) for the Snetterton team's tea in 1925 - with the tea ladies, vital to any club, well to the fore. Standing proudly in the middle and padded up is the captain, William Smith, and behind him is "Chalker" Jessup. In those days they nearly all had nicknames! Eccles, Hockham, Rockland and Shropham figured among the opposition. Away grounds were reached by means of waggon, bicycle or shanks's pony. Members of grander clubs may have had a car or two, while longer journeys were often made by train.

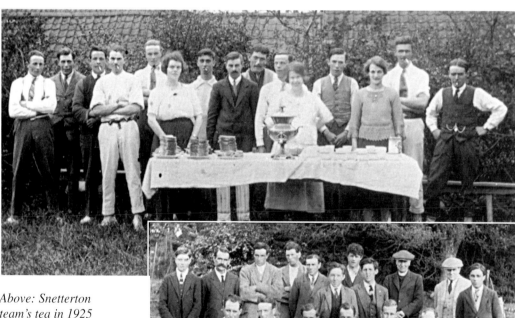

Above: Snetterton team's tea in 1925

Right: The Shelton team of about 1924

The Shelton team c.1924 (previous page, lower right) assemble during the interval for tea at Shelton Hall, home of the Hawkins family. Edward Hawkins is second from the right in the back row and Lieutenant Commander Richard Hawkins is seated second from the right. Like the local squire, who often provided the field, the local parson took a great interest in the cricket team and, at Shelton, the Rev. Charles Swainson was no exception. Several members of the Hubbard family formed the backbone of the Shelton team.

Cups and Shields

BY THE Twenties there was keen competition for various trophies, the most important of which were the Senior Cup, founded in 1884, and the Saturday Junior Cup, commenced in 1891. There was also a Thursday Junior Cup.

In the Mid-Norfolk League, founded in 1898, better village teams competed for the Mid-Norfolk League Challenge Shield, whilst teams in the lower divisions and 2nd XIs played for the Boyle Cup. The Shield competition had been instituted in 1904 and the Cup had been presented by W. L. Boyle M.P. in 1911. These competitions still run today.

In North Norfolk, teams were playing for the North Norfolk Village Shield, while in the East Norfolk League, formed in 1906, the Falcon Cup was the trophy to win.

There were other competitions, among them the Cromer District League, the Sandringham and District League and the Wicklewood and District League.

The Thetford team which defeated Mattishall 137-5 against 98 in the final of the 1928 Norfolk (Saturday) Junior Cup. The Thetford team included several L.N.E.R. railway employees and the picture was taken on the Recreation Ground at Mundford Road in the town. Holding the cup is the captain Alfred Le Grys, who in the first round had hammered 118 runs in 80 minutes off the Caley's Recreation bowlers.

The Hethersett team which won the final of the Norfolk (Saturday) Junior Cup at Lakenham in 1929. In that match Hethersett totalled 155-9 to the 77 of Yarmouth Exiles. Walter Dann (second from left in the back row) made a spectacular 102 not out, while J. A. Read (second from left in the middle row) took eight Yarmouth wickets for 36 runs.

The successful Mileham club of 1920. In that year the first team beat Watt's Naval Training School 101-61 to win the Mid-Norfolk Shield and the 2nd XI secured a 59 to 53 win over Wendling to take the Boyle Cup. Over 500 people watched the Shield Final at Sennowe Park and the Mileham innings was built round William Cason (eighth from the left in the back row) who top-scored with 26. Mileham retained the Shield in the years 1921-1923 inclusive.

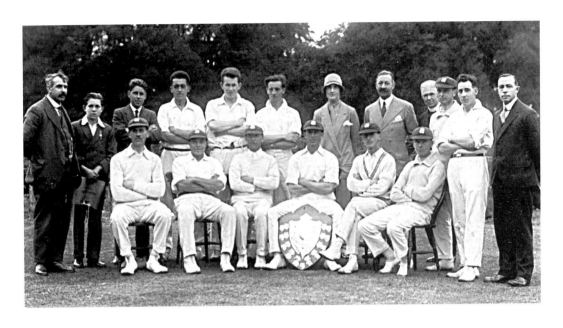

Melton Park and Swanton Novers C.C. when they defeated Field Dalling in the final of the North Norfolk Village Cricket League Shield at Melton Park in 1927. Sitting behind the Shield is the captain E. Leeder.

The finals were played in the Park and Lord Hastings, who presented the Shield, together with Lady Hastings, took a great interest in local cricket. They are in the back row. In the evening a celebratory dinner was held at the Melton Constable Railway Institute. The Melton team also won the Shield in 1929 and 1935 on the former occasion pipping Field Dalling by just two runs in the final.

Lord Hastings ensured the Park Cricket Ground was well maintained and when the pitch was rolled, the horses pulling the roller wore pads on their feet.

The magnificent South Norfolk Village Cricket League Challenge Cup. It was presented by Lionel Robinson on the formation of the League in 1920. The first winners were Pulham, who held it four times in the Twenties, and the last were Hingham in 1931.

Schoolboy Greats

THIS photo-graph of the 1929 Norwich School XI, coming out to field, shows the Cathedral as a beautiful backdrop to a typical English scene. Many talented cricketers have been nurtured at the School, among them Basil Cozens-Hardy before he moved to Rugby School, Geoffrey Stevens, Bryan Stevens and Clive Radley.

Other schools, particularly Gresham's, produced their share of skilful players and in the late Twenties, Bertram "George" Clements, who became a valuable all-rounder for Norfolk, was learning his trade at the City of Norwich School. However, Bracondale's contribution must not be overlooked, for several of the famous Edrich clan passed through that seat of learning. In the photograph, taken in May 1929, of the Bracondale 1st XI, the great W. J. "Bill" Edrich is sitting on the grass second from the left. Born at Lingwood in 1916, it was in the Thirties that Bill's cricketing prowess brought a meteoric rise to fame. Third from the left in the back row is Gordon Fitt, who found national fame in another sport - tennis.

Chapter Four

Great Times in the Thirties

The brilliant David Walker (left) and Cedric Thistleton-Smith coming out to bat for Norfolk after the tea interval on the second day of the 1933 Challenge Match against Yorkshire II.

The Australians at Sandringham

O N A Sunday afternoon in June 1930, the Australian touring party were received by King George V and Queen Mary at Sandringham, where they were shown round.

On the left in the picture, talking to the King, is the tourist's captain and opening batsman William Woodfull, while on the extreme right is Victor Richardson, the vice-captain and an attacking middle order batsman. Between Richardson and the Queen is Mr. W. L. Kelly, the Australian manager. While the tourists were at Sandringham, word spread in the locality and a large crowd gathered to give them a rousing welcome.

Before going to meet the King and Queen, the Australians had been entertained to lunch by Viscount and Viscountess Downe at Hillington Hall. Later in the afternoon, on returning to the Hall for tea, they met the village cricketers of Flitcham and Hillington on the pitch in Hillington Park. Clarrie Grimmett, the famous leg break and googly bowler, spent some time showing the local lads how to bowl.

Norfolk County Cricket Club's Golden Era

T HE Norfolk County team made an inauspicious start to the Thirties, though they did entertain the New Zealand and Indian tourists. The match against New Zealand in 1931 was lost by an innings and 62 runs, while that against All India in 1932 by 128 runs. But even in these heavy reverses there were encouraging signs of good times ahead.

Michael Falcon leads the Norfolk team out at Lakenham in 1931. Left to right: J. C. Thistleton-Smith, J. M.Coldham, M. Falcon, D. F. Walker, G. N. Scott-Chadd, N. L. Foster, B. W. Rought-Rought, W. G. Eagle, D. C. Rought-Rought

In the first innings of the match with New Zealand, David Walker, the 18 year old Uppingham School captain who was making his third appearance for the county, went in first wicket down and carried his bat for 31 as Norfolk were shot out for 97. Then against All India, W. J. "Bill" Edrich, then 16 years old and making his debut, scored 20 out of Norfolk's total of 49 in the first innings and 16 in the second. Young Edrich faced the formidable pace bowling of Mahomed Nissar, who had match figures of 14-57, and Wisden commented: "Edrich, a schoolboy, batted in promising fashion for Norfolk."

Norfolk and All India at Lakenham in 1932. Bill Edrich is sitting on the extreme right in the front row

If there was a Golden Age for Norfolk County Cricket Club, it was surely the mid-Thirties. In the seasons 1933-36, the County did not lose a single Minor Counties match, always finishing in the top three in the table.

Bill Edrich played until the 1936 season, before a permanent move to Middlesex, and he produced great performances with both bat and ball. The brilliant Walker topped the batting averages for seven seasons in the 1930s, scoring 651 runs in 1934 at a phenomenal average of 93.00. Michael Falcon was, of course, captain of this successful side, which also boasted Tristan Ballance, a telling left arm slow bowler who, like Walker, was also an Oxford blue. The contribution of the Rought-Rought brothers was crucial, while

Tristan Ballance, Norfolk's brilliant slow bowler of the 1930s. He was also a useful batsman and a brilliant fielder

that spectacular big hitter and fast bowler Wilfrid Thompson and Cedric Thistleton-Smith also played their parts. Thistleton-Smith scored a magnificent 174 in an away fixture with Cambridgeshire in 1933, but perhaps his finest innings was when opening against Kent II at Tonbridge in 1934, he was still there on 95 not out when Norfolk won the match with two wickets to spare.

In this vintage period the year 1933 stands out. Norfolk topped the Minor Counties table, but had to face Yorkshire II, who were placed second, in the traditional Challenge Match at

Norfolk's 1933 Challenge Match Team. Standing (l to r): D. G. Buxton (Hon. Sec.), W. S. Thompson, D. C. Rought-Rought, R. C. Rought-Rought, B. J. Wood, T. G. L. Ballance, F. D. Cunliffe. Sitting (l to r): W. J. Edrich, B. W. Rought-Rought, M. Falcon (capt.), D. F. Walker, J. C. Thistleton-Smith

Col. R. C. J. Chichester-Constable leads Yorkshire II out at Lakenham in the 1933 Challenge Match. Immediately behind the captain are W. E. Harbord, (extreme right) and N. W. D. Yardley (3rd from right). Len Hutton can just be seen 5th from right at the back

Michael Falcon leads out Norfolk during the 1933 Challenge Match. W. S. Thompson is on the extreme left with D. C. Rought-Rought behind Falcon. D. F. Walker is second from the right in front of the hidden player with R. C. Rought-Rought on the extreme right

MINOR COUNTIES CHALLENGE MATCH.

NORFOLK COUNTY CRICKET CLUB

NORFOLK v. YORKSHIRE II.

September 6th, 7th & 8th, 1933.

NORFOLK 1st Innings.		NORFOLK—2nd Innings.	
1 B. W. Rought-Rought lbw b Hall	1	b Hall	0
2 D. F. Walker b Heaton	10	c Buller b Hall	53
3 W. J. Edrich b Hall	0	st Buller b Heaton	3
4 *M. Falcon b Heaton	45	c Douglas b Heaton	11
5 J. C. Thornton-Smith b Hall	24	b Hall	8
6 D. C. Rought-Rought c & b Heaton	35	c Douglas b Heaton	19
7 F. D. Cunliffe st Buller b Heaton	21	st Buller b Heaton	2
8 W. S. Thompson st Buller b Heaton	2	st Buller b Heaton	0
9 R. C. Rought-Rought b Douglas	2	st Buller b Heaton	12
10 †B. J. Wood b Douglas	2	b Hall	6
11 T. G. L. Ballance not out	0	not out	3
Extras	5	Extras	5
Total	147	Total	122

Wkts.	1	2	3	4	5	6	7	8	9	10	1	2	3	4	5	6	7	8	9	10
Runs	1	25	60	68	124	126	133	141	147		6	42	75	83	92	92	99	118	122	

YORKSHIRE II.—1st Innings.		YORKSHIRE II. 2nd Innings.	
1 Hutton c Walker b R. C. R.-Rought	34	not out	16
2 K. R. Davidson c Wood b R. C. R.-Rought	59	c Wood b R. C. R.-Rought	1
3 W. E. Harbord c Wood b Thompson	36	not out	24
4 Turner b R. C. R.-Rought	51		
5 N. W. D. Yardley c Wood b D. C. R.-Rought	23		
6 Pearson c Walker b D. C. R.-Rought	0		
7 †Buller b D. C. R.-Rought	4		
8 Heaton run out	0		
*9 Col. R. C. Chichester-Constable b R. R.-Rought	7		
10 Douglas not out	0		
11 Hall run out	0		
Extras	14	Extras	1
Total	230	Total	42

Wkts.	1	2	3	4	5	6	7	8	9	10	1	2	3	4	5	6	7	8	9	10
Runs	94	99	168	212	212	221	221	221	225	230	1									

* Captain.   † Wicket-keeper.   Umpires : Hubble & Tyler.

Tos won by Norfolk.

Applications for membership of the County Cricket Club should be sent to the
Hon. Secretary, Catton Hall, Norwich.

PRINTED ON THE GROUND BY T. G. ELLIS 62 WEST POTTERGATE NORWICH

Lakenham. The Yorkshire second string included Norman Yardley, later to captain England, and a young Pudsey lad called Len Hutton. Thus the match provided the first of many encounters this pair would have with Norfolk's own Bill Edrich. Disappointingly, the all-amateur Norfolk team, which included five University blues, not to mention Edrich, did not do themselves justice and lost to a Yorkshire team, which boasted seven professionals, by nine wickets. Yorkshire were champions, but not for long. Later, when the Minor Counties table was checked for insertion in Wisden, it was found that Wiltshire should have been placed second and so challenged Norfolk. Thus the Challenge Match result was disregarded and, for 1933, the championship was declared "not decided".

In 1933, Norfolk entertained the West Indies and the great George Headley made a monumental 257 not out for the tourists. The West Indies led by 239 on the first innings, but the match was drawn. Then in 1935, before 10,000 spectators at Lakenham, Norfolk excelled themselves against the South Africans. In their first innings, the County made 325 - a score not bettered against the touring team by any first-class county that season. Edrich, by then on the M.C.C. groundstaff, hit a magnificent 111, receiving good support from Michael Barton, who made 59. Later in 1948, Barton, another Oxford blue, left Norfolk to play for Surrey, whom he captained for a spell.

Schoolboys look on in awe as the great George Headley (left) goes to the wicket with Clifford Roach to resume the West Indies' innings at Lakenham in 1933

Michael Barton, Norfolk's Oxford University Blue who went on to captain Surrey

In the three seasons before the War, Norfolk dropped to almost a mid-table position, but one memorable occasion occurred at Lakenham in August 1939. David Walker (217) and Harold

Norfolk County Cricket Club

NORFOLK v. NORTHUMBERLAND
WEDNESDAY & THURSDAY, AUGUST 16th & 17th, 1939

NORFOLK—1st Innings.   NORFOLK.—2nd Innings

1 D. F. Walker c Robson H. b Ramsden ..	217	
2 H. E. Theobald lbw b Ramsden	93	
3 B. W. Rought-Rought		
4 Edrich (G. A.) not out	17	
5 *E. H. Edrich b Robson H.	19	
6 *M. Falcon		
7 W. S. Thompson b Robson H.	7	
8 G. R. Langdale		
9 R. Leggett not out	19	
10 Boswell		
11 Lingwood		

Extras 16   Extras

Total (4 wkts. dec.) 385   Total

Wkts. 1 2 3 4 5 6 7 8 9 10   1 2 3 4 5 6 7 8 9 10
Runs 323 323 342 355

BOWLING ANALYSIS.—First Innings.

		O.	M.	R	W		Second Innings. O.	M.	R	W
Allan	...	23	3	170	0		—	—	—	—
Robson H.	...	29	3	158	2		—	—	—	—
T. Robson	...	2	—	15			—	—	—	—
Davey	...	7	—	40	—		—	—	—	—
Newman	...	4	—	32	—		—	—	—	—
Ramsden		1	—	7	2		—	—	—	—

NORTHUMBERLAND 1st Innings   N'THUMBERLAND 2nd. Inns

1 W. G. Mackay c E. Edrich b Boswell	...	18	b Thompson	6
2 I. Murray c Walker b Thompson	...	1	c E. Edrich b Langdale	15
3 A. D. Ramsden c E. Edrich b Thompson	...	0	b Thompson	0
4 H. C. Lee lbw b Boswell	...	12	c E. Edrich b Lingwood	1
5 P. Vaulkard c E. Edrich b Edrich G.	...	17	c Langdale b Boswell	25
6 N. A. Newman c E. Edrich b Edrich G.	...	3	lbw b Boswell	4
7 M. Davey not out	...	56	c Boswell b Langdale	0
8 *T. A. W. White c Falcon b Boswell	...	0	b Langdale	
9 T. Robson c E. Edrich b Langdale	...	46		
10 Robson (H.) c Lingwood b Thompson	...	21		
11 J. L. Allan lbw b Thompson	...	0		

Extras 10   Extras

Total 196   Total 136

Wkts. 1 2 3 4 5 6 7 8 9 10   1 2 3 4 5 6 7 8 9 10
Runs. 3 3 41 50 64 64 67 136 196 196   13 14 19 35 35 40 59 63 121

BOWLING ANALYSIS.—First Innings.

		O.	M.	R.	W.		Second Innings. O.	M	R.	W
Thompson	...	10.6	—	38	4		Thompson —	—	—	—
Lingwood	...	8	1	35	—		Lingwood —	—	—	—
Boswell	...	12	—	67	3		Boswell —	—	—	—
Edrich G.	...	9	2	35	2		Langdale —	—	—	—
Langdale	...	3	—	11	1		

* Captain † Wicketkeeper   Umpires: Canning & Cutler   Toss won by Norfolk.

Printed on the Ground by T. G. ELLIS, 62, West Pottergate, Norwich.

Theobald (93) put on 323 for the first wicket against Northumberland, breaking the record set up by the brothers Jarvis in 1885. The partnership of 323 still stands as a Norfolk record for any wicket.

The New Zealand tourists visited Lakenham in 1937 and defeated Norfolk, but in 1939 the County overhauled the West Indies' total to finish a drawn game on 375-9. Harold Theobald scored 70 and Geoffrey Edrich chipped in with 53.

Above: The scorecard recording a famous first wicket partnership.

Left: Norfolk coming out to field in 1939. In front are Falcon, Walker and Harold Theobald. C. S. R. Boswell is on the extreme left and the wicket-keeper is Eric Edrich

Both Geoffrey Edrich and his brother Eric, a wicket-keeper batsman, were now valued members of the Norfolk side, but after the War they would enter the professional game with Lancashire, though Eric would return to Norfolk in 1949. Sadly Ballance and Walker, those brightest stars of the 1930s, were to lose their lives on active service during the hostilities.

Jack Nichols takes a team to Wymondham

ONE of the highlights of the Wymondham Cricket Club season in the early 1930s was the annual visit to the town's King's Head Meadow of an XI assembled by John E. "Jack" Nichols, then the County coach.

As a boy, Nichols had practised cricketing skills on that very same field in Wymondham, where his father lived. Developing into a useful all-rounder, he turned out for Norfolk in 1898, then had a handful of games for Worcestershire, before enjoying a successful Minor Counties career with first Staffordshire and then Norfolk (1921-1931). From 1932 to 1938, he was engaged as Norfolk coach and during that period, when visiting his father, he used to advise the Wymondham players in the nets. In 1935 he prepared, free of expense, a marl wicket on the King's Head Meadow.

Below: Jack Nichols's XI and Wymondham C.C. before their 1932 encounter. Nichols is seated on the bench third from the left. Further along are the young Edrich brothers, Geoffrey and Bill, wearing Bracondale School blazers. Lingwood, the County Professional, is sitting on the ground on the left and behind him, padded up, is Freddie Self. Ballance and Clements are third and seventh from the left in the middle row.

Above: Dr. G. C. Gaynor and W. P. Hall go out to open the Wymondham innings against Nichols's XI on the King's Head Meadow

Fast bowler Norman Brighton steaming in against Nichols's XI

The accompanying pictures come from the match in August 1932 when Nichols brought to Wymondham a particularly strong side. Among those included were T. G. Ballance, B. A. Clements, W. J. Lingwood, F. G. Self, together with the Edrich brothers, Bill and Geoffrey. All would play for the County. Then aged 16, Bill Edrich hit 66 not out (including ten 4's and two 6's) in a total of 103-5 declared, but Wymondham's Norman Brighton took 4-7 in ten overs. It was a fine performance by the town youngster, who went on to make quite a reputation in local cricket circles as a fast left arm round the wicket bowler. Wymondham mustered only 44, Lingwood taking 6-17.

In the following season's game, Wymondham were again dismissed for 44, this time in reply to 163-4 declared. For the winners, Freddie Self made 31, but W. J. Edrich was again undefeated with 73. Without the great W.J. in the 1934 match, a tie resulted with both teams totalling 65.

The Great Days of the East Norfolk Club

AMONG personalities in this picture of a side representing the East Norfolk Club in the 1930s are, on the back row, Brigadier "Boy" Clowes and Jack Borrett, third and fourth from the left. Of those sitting, Walter Dann is in the middle and Sir Frederick Rawlinson is on the right. For a time, Sir Frederick was the club secretary.

Just as the South Norfolk Club had reached its zenith in the 1920s, so East Norfolk did in the 1930s. The majority of the team's fixtures were played on the delightful ground at Smallburgh Hall, home of Thomas Wolsey. Visitors included Cambridge University Crusaders, Notts Forest and Eton Ramblers. On occasions, trips were made to places as far afield as Bath and Chippenham.

Matches were usually all-day affairs, but there were some of a two-day duration. The strength of the side varied from game to game, probably depending on the opposition. Sometimes County players of the calibre of Michael Falcon and Harold Theobald were brought into service. But rivals West Norfolk included the Edrich brothers, Eric and Geoffrey, and could call on R. A. A. Beresford, his son Richard Marcus, and later Rufus Leggett - all County standard.

In the late Thirties, the East Norfolk Club seems to have been troubled by various administrative difficulties and there were disappointments. In July 1937, a two-day game was staged at Smallburgh against the famous Sir Julien Cahn's XI. Although including batsmen like Tom Reddick (later Nottinghamshire) and Harold Mudge (New South Wales), the visitors were dismissed for 78. However with former South African test player Robert Crisp bowling, East Norfolk were all out for 48 runs. Rain caused the abandonment of the second day's play, but there then followed an unsavoury dispute over the expenses for Sir Julien's team and its supporters, particularly in relation to the cost of lunches and teas.

A further set-back occurred in 1938 when a much awaited visit by the touring Rajputana Club from India was cancelled at a late date, because of failure to reach agreement over the financial arrangements.

With the outbreak of hostilities in 1939, the East Norfolk Club folded and their blazers were acquired by Norwich Natives C.C.

Clubs in the News

THE Clenchwarton team pictured on a red-letter day in 1937 when they beat a powerful Hucknall side, including some ex-professionals, on the Nottingham University Ground. Clenchwarton made 110, while in reply Hucknall could only muster 40 - thanks largely to some fine pace bowling by Fred Boon, who took 8-18. Reporting the match, the Nottingham Evening Post carried the headline: "He bowls like Larwood."

In the front row of the photograph are R. Carlin (second from left) from Hucknall, U. N. Myall (third from left) who played a great part in running the club, Fred Boon (fourth from left) and Col Coates (extreme right). Coates made his debut in 1923 and played his last game in 1974 at the age of 65 when he batted right

through the innings. Another great supporter of the club for well over 70 years was Charles Collison (second from left in the back row).

Ashmanhaugh seen when they won the Saturday Junior Cup in 1933, the year in which they also took the Falcon Cup. They won the Junior Cup again in 1936 and 1938.

In the 1936 final at Lakenham, H. G. "Bill" Abbs (seated first from the right) scored 77 not out as Ashmanhaugh beat Colton 132-27. E. Blanch (second from the

left in the back row) took 7-11. Abbs later captained the side, but in 1946 he moved to Mildenhall and gave the club there sterling service for many years.

The tea interval during a match between Martham and a representative side from the rest of the George Beck League around 1938. Among the opposition were players from Fleggburgh and Rollesby.

From the mid-1920s, Martham played on Starling's Meadow, where this picture was taken. Oliver Starling and his wife are on the extreme right, while the man fifth from the right, with a pipe, is Ossie Larter. In one match in the Thirties, Larter hit a century for Martham - a rare feat bearing in mind the height of the grass. He had to hit the ball in the air and at tea was 83 not out. The Martham captain declined to make the customary declaration at the interval and allowed Larter to bat on after the break to reach his hundred.

Sheringham C.C. pictured on Whit-Monday 1939 during an all-day game against the City of Norwich Poor Law Officials. Sheringham defeated the Poor Law Officials by an innings and 31 runs; and their own total of 178 was almost entirely due to Freddie Sayer (98) and Roy Brownsell (61). Sayer is second from the left in the front row with Brownsell fourth from  the left. Between them is Alec Youngs, the captain, while the man in the back row wearing a trilby is W. J. Nunn, the club secretary. Among the spectators at the match was Stanley Christopherson, then President of the M.C.C., who had once resided in the town.

The Sheringham Club had been reformed in 1936 after a period of lapse and, in the years preceding the War, it enjoyed regular fixtures with the 17th Anti- Aircraft Battery stationed at Weybourne Camp. Late in the 1939 season Sheringham were able to call on G. Guest, who was stationed nearby with the R.A.F., and in a game against Mundesley he became the first player in the club's history to score a century.

The successful Thornham team proudly posing in 1939 after they had won both the Sandringham and District League Cup and the League twenty-over knockout shield. Holding the trophies is the captain Eddie Bell. The cup and medals were presented by Mr H. E. Wharton, the League's President, after an exciting win over Hillington at Hunstanton by 104-103. For Thornham, "Laddie" Frohawk took 6-43. Thornham had also been League Champions the previous two years as well as taking the Shield in 1938.

The League Championship dated from 1910, the first winners being Wolferton, but the knockout competition was not started until 1937 when Major F. G. Thorne presented the Shield. In 1928, the Major had also donated a shield for the Division II winners and this was played for until 1980.

Sadly, the League, which once included the likes of Castle Rising, Dersingham and Heacham, was disbanded in 1992. This was due to some clubs folding, but more importantly to the rise of the West Norfolk League.

Dereham Cricket Club in 1934, seven years after its new pavilion had been opened by Michael Falcon. In a match to celebrate the occasion, Dereham beat Norfolk Ramblers by 172-8 declared to 88. The pavilion replaced an old railway carriage on the Norwich Road ground, where Dereham had played since 1904.

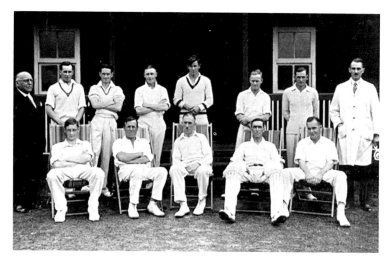

By 1934, Freddie Masters, third from the right in the back row, had a regular first team place. He had made his debut for the Second XI in 1926 and was still playing for the "A" team in 1976! One of his many memorable matches was that in July 1939, when Heacham, who had been unbeaten in their previous twelve matches that season, visited Dereham and were thrashed 127-49. Masters took 7-21, including the prized wickets of the Edrich brothers, Geoffrey and Eric, both of whom had been in commanding form that year.

Top scorer for Dereham in that Heacham match was Alexander Barton, seen on the extreme left of those seated in the photograph. A cousin of Michael Barton, he was principally a slow bowler and had a few games for Norfolk, but tragically he was killed on active service. Second from the left in the back row is W. J. Hicks, who found fame as a sports journalist with newspapers, like the Daily Mail and the B.B.C.

Jardine meets the locals at Buckenham Tofts

BUCKENHAM Tofts lies in what has been known since 1942 as the Stanford Battle Area, but in the Thirties it saw some exciting cricket. Living at Buckenham Tofts Hall in the late 1930s was Edward Steane-Price, who was President of the village club which played on the well-maintained ground in his Park. The cricket field was even surrounded by netting to protect it from rabbits, so prevalent in Breckland.

In 1934, Douglas Jardine, England's captain during the infamous Bodyline Tests, married Irene Margaret Peat, the daughter of Sir Harry Peat of Hockwold Hall, which is also in the Breckland. So it was that in the 1930s, Sir Harry Peat's XI, captained by Jardine, would pay an annual visit to Buckenham Tofts Park to play the local village side.

The most notable match between the teams took place in July 1937 before about 300 spectators. Buckenham Tofts batted first and totalled 146, of which 102 were scored in a brilliant attacking innings by George Goss, the captain, who hit eight 6's and five 4's. The next highest innings was that of Reg Boyce, who made 11. At the close of the home club's innings, tea was served in a marquee on the Park, to which Mr Steane-Price invited both teams to join his guests. When Sir Harry Peat's XI went in, they lost Colin McIver, the Essex player, with the score at 36, but went on to reach 207 for the loss of three wickets. Scoring freely all round the ground, Jardine made 97 not out. At the end of the match, the former England captain recognised Goss's achievement in producing such an explosive innings against experienced bowlers by presenting the local hero with the ball. It was an occasion the home players would always remember and the ball, with a silver band attached and suitably engraved, is still cherished by Goss's grandson today.

The next year, Sir Harry's XI included not only Jardine, but that wonderful all-rounder Percy Fender. Buckenham Tofts were all out for 63 and Sir Harry's team replied with 136, Jardine contributing 32. For the village team, R. Bell took 4-36 and Ken Allington 2-17. Allington recalls once bagging Jardine and Fender with successive deliveries; and this may have been the occasion. In any event, the

Buckenham Tofts star bowler was again in form the following week, when he took 8-7 against less distinguished opposition - Cockley Cley.

Buckenham Tofts in the 1930s. Ken Allington, a spinner, is holding the ball on the right at the front

The Edrich Family XI captures the public's imagination

So unique was the match in which an Edrich family XI played Michael Falcon's Norfolk XI in September 1938 that it attracted nationwide interest and the B.B.C. sent a team along to broadcast it on the wireless. An All-Edrich XI had played a drawn game against East Norfolk in 1931, which had been curtailed by the weather, but since then Bill had established himself as a first-class cricketer who was making Test appearances, while Eric and Geoffrey were playing in the Norfolk County side. Indeed, in 1938, Bill had achieved the great feat of scoring 1000 first-class runs before the end of May.

The match was the idea of the Rev. A. Shillito, the Rector of Blofield, who saw it as a means of raising funds for the Recreation Ground. But the game proved a big anti-climax. The weather was unkind and, batting in the rain, Falcon's XI made 132 for the loss of two wickets before declaring, Harold Theobald scoring 61 with some big hitting. The crowd were full of anticipation when Bill accompanied his father to the wicket to begin the family's reply. He received the first ball from George Pilch and there were gasps of amazement as he

The Edrich XI at Blofield in 1938. Left to right: George C., George H., Edwin H., Arthur, Harry M., Geoffrey A., Brian R., Eric H., Alan W., William A., William J. (captain)

touched it into the hands of Rodney Rought-Rought in the slips. The great W. J. was out for "0" and one national newspaper carried the headline: "Local boy doesn't make good."

Only Eric with 39 not out did himself justice as the family team slumped to 65-6 before the rain called a final halt to the proceedings.

About a week later, the Edrich XI again took the field, this time at Barton Hall, the home of a flamboyant character called Michael Trubshawe. The family faced Norfolk Bitterns, who fielded a strong side including seven County players, but on this occasion the Edriches won with ease. Bill scored a sparkling century and Brian, who had recently turned 16 and would later play for Kent, made a splendid 73.

In the following winter, after a series of Test failures on the South African tour, Bill scored 219 in the final "Timeless Test" at Durban. Then at the end of the 1939 English season, war broke out and from a cricket hero, he became a wartime hero winning the D.F.C. as a bomber pilot.

The Edrich XI and Norfolk Bitterns at Barton Hall in 1938. Michael Trubshawe (with dog) sits between Bill and Eric Edrich. Among the family's opposition were J. C. Thistleton-Smith (third from right, middle row), and Harold Theobald (second from right, front row). The umpire on the left at the back is Jack Nichols

Chapter Five

Post War until the Sixties

Eric Edrich (left) and Geoffrey, his brother, going out to bat for A. J. Borrett's team against Dereham in September 1947. At the time, both were professionals with Lancashire. From 1942 to 1945, Geoffrey had endured a harsh time at the hands of the Japanese..

Revival in the Late Forties

IN the drive to increase food production during the War, the lovely Green at Aldborough had been ploughed up. This picture was taken in 1947 when the village team were due to play their first match after the Green had been re-levelled. The opposition never turned up, so the

Aldborough lads just posed for the photographer. In 1951, Aldborough won the North Norfolk Village Shield and in 1954 the Rothermere Cup.

Jack Borrett leads his team out at Dereham in 1947. W. J. "Bill" Edrich is at the front on the right, Geoffrey Edrich is fifth from the left and wicket-keeper Eric Edrich is on the extreme left

In September 1947, straight after a decisive win at Lakenham by the Edrich family XI over G. E. Pilch's XI, when Eric scored 129 and Bill 49, several of the family appeared for A. J. Borrett's team against Dereham. The Dereham club charged 1/- (5p) admission and must have been pleased with the gate of nearly 2000. Geoff Edrich scored 67 and brother Eric 81, before Borrett declared at 206-7. Dereham bowler F. T. Marsh took a creditable 4-40, including the wicket of the illustrious W.J. Dereham were then dismissed for 85.

Big John Edwards (third from the right), a local baker, leading Harleston out to field in a home match against Ingham in the Forties. Under his leadership Harleston assembled a

strong team, including County player Frank Cunliffe (wearing cap) and Doug Mattocks (extreme right). Until a new pavilion was built, the dressing-room was the upper floor of the barn seen in the background.

Although Norwich Wanderers had been founded in 1913, it was not until 1948 that they had a home ground at Barton Turf - hence the name "Wanderers." The picture shows Mr W. 0. Copeman, the Club President (left), and Mr. J. S. Redmayne at the ground's opening.

King George VI opened Sandringham's new pavilion on 1st July 1950 after he had generously arranged for it to be speedily built following a fire which had destroyed the old one the previous year. The King, accompanied by the Queen and Princess Margaret, stayed to see D. Boughen (fourth from the right in the back row, previous page) finish with figures of 8-21 as the visiting R.A.F. team from West Raynham were dismissed for 34. During the Sandringham Estate cottage horticultural show the next year, the King watched some of Sandringham's match with West Norfolk, which was played on the same day.

The Lakenham Scene in the Early Fifties

A LTHOUGH there were some fine individual performances by the likes of Brian Clements, Eric Edrich and Peter Powell, there was little to cheer about for Norfolk supporters in the post-war period. That Norfolk's win over Suffolk by an innings and 46 runs in 1952 was the County's first victory for three years proves the point. However, in that match, that great stalwart C. S. R. Boswell took 5-8 in Suffolk's first innings, while the youthful Peter Walmsley had match figures of 10-57. The year 1955 saw Peter Parfitt and Nigel Moore averaging over 57 and 53 respectively with the bat, but perhaps the main spectator-interest in the early 1950s was occasioned by visits from the touring sides to Lakenham to play the Minor Counties' XI.

Right: Sonny Ramadhin approached by autograph hunters at Lakenham in 1950.

Left: The West Indies go out to field at Lakenham in 1950

In 1950 and 1951, the Minor Counties suffered heavy innings defeats against the West Indies and the South Africans, while the 1952 match against the Indians was drawn. But these games gave Norfolk devotees the chance to admire test stars like Jack Cheetham, who hit an attractive 114 not out for the South Africans, and that little wizard Sonny Ramadhin who took 7-33 for the West Indies in the Minor Counties' first innings.

Prolific batsman Eric Rowan (third from left) leads the South Africans out at Lakenham in 1951

Norfolk v. Hertfordshire at Lakenham in August 1954. Norfolk won the match by 84 runs

The Club Scene

HORSFORD'S pavilion at Manor Park was officially opened in May 1951 by Michael Falcon, who then led the home team to an 18-run victory over a Hoveton and Wroxham side. From the time of this picture (overleaf) in the mid-1950s, the Wilkinson family made a big contribution to Horsford's climb to the top echelons of local cricket. Back row (left to

right): Malcolm Wilkinson, Derek Godfrey, Gordon Godfrey, Jim Townsend, Tony Watson, Mervyn Wilkinson. Front row (left to right): Marcus Wilkinson, Wilfred Wilkinson, Don Rayner, Horace Bowman, Ken Smith (wicket-keeper).

Overstrand pictured in 1953 when they enjoyed their most successful season, winning 21 out of 35 matches. Huge victories over local rivals Cromer and Sheringham during the August Bank Holiday weekend were the icing on the cake. Peter Ryder, the captain sitting fourth from the left in the front row, proved a more than useful spinner and topped the batting with 794 runs (average 33.1). Pace man Brian Thetford (seated second from the left) headed the bowling with 72 wickets (average 7.2).

Rackheath and their supporters during a home fixture at Sprowston Grange in 1955. They took tea in the Grange, which also provided a changing-room. Eddie Symonds (extreme left) is preparing to pad up, while Norman Dunger (seated with glasses) has already done so.

Gifted left-hander George Mason batting for Dereham at Bradenham in the early 1960s. Before moving to Dereham halfway through the 1960 season, Mason had played for Burnham Thorpe, Burnham Market and Hunstanton. With the likes of Derek Chamberlain, John Parfitt and Barry Battelley, he could keep the Dereham score moving quickly on a good day. Tragically his premature death occurred at the age of 41.

The Mulbarton and Swardeston team which won the Kimberley Cup in 1965 defeating Wymondham in the final by five runs. Veteran captain Maurice Wadsley is holding the bat. The club, which changed its name to Swardeston in 1974, won the cup in numerous later seasons. The Kimberley Cup competition was instituted in 1935.

This 1968 Norwich Union team, captained by Roy Leathers, contained four players with County experience - Mike Oxbury and David Stockings, second and fourth from the left at the back, Peter Walmsley and Geoff Fiddler, second and fourth from the left at the front. Fiddler and Stockings were batsman, while Oxbury and the formidable Walmsley were quickies. That season Leathers led the Union run-makers.

Occasions

*Peter Softley (Norfolk) bowling to E. W. Swanton, the famous cricket writer,
(F. G. Mann's XI) at Lakenham in 1951. Swanton made 53 in the first innings*

Special matches were staged to celebrate the Festival of Britain in 1951 and, at Lakenham, Norfolk played an XI raised by F. G. Mann, the former Middlesex and England skipper. Although a fair-sized crowd enjoyed some admirable cricket, the two-day match was drawn with Mann's XI scoring 334-8 declared (Mann 85, Viscount Cobham 78 not out, Rudd 58, E. W. Swanton 53) and 149-9 declared to Norfolk's 255-9 declared and 192-7. At Eaton Park,

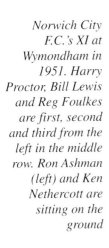

Norwich City F.C.'s XI at Wymondham in 1951. Harry Proctor, Bill Lewis and Reg Foulkes are first, second and third from the left in the middle row. Ron Ashman (left) and Ken Nethercott are sitting on the ground

Norwich, twenty-over knockout competitions were held for Junior and Senior clubs, while a Norwich City F.C. XI, with Ken Nethercott keeping wicket, visited Wymondham to play the locals in a game for which there was an admission charge of 6d (2 1/2p). It was all good stuff.

Wymondham's Festival of Britain team - back row, left to right: Mr. Burgess, Dr. N. Lees, K. Percival, A. Halstead, J. Cantley, ____; Middle row: S. Canham, A. Harwood, H. Childerhouse, S. Cavill; Front row: A. Banham, N. Brighton, I. Sheldrake

This photograph was taken on 30th August 1952 - a memorable day in the history of the Pulhams' Cricket Club. Peter Baker, then M.P. for South Norfolk who is shown padded up, brought a team of parliamentary and business colleagues to play the local side. The Pulhams batted first and made 108, Henry Staff, second from the right of those sitting on the grass, top-scoring with 25. Peter Baker's XI then reached 123-7, but Charles Mott-Radclyffe, sitting first left on the grass and later prominent in Norfolk County C.C. affairs, failed to trouble the scorers. Sitting second left on the grass is William Rees-Mogg, later Lord Rees-Mogg. Mr Baker and his friends had entertained the locals to lunch at the King's Head Inn.

A happy gathering of members of Dereham Cricket Club after the opening of their new pavilion, costing £800, in May 1953. The ceremony was performed by Rowland Hill, the club's secretary from 1921-1933, during a match in which Dereham 107-6 (F. Cooke 59) defeated Norwich Wanderers 103 (J. Cooke 6-46) by four wickets. The previous building had been destroyed by fire in 1943. After the opening, acting-captain Claude Cordle (seated first on the left in the middle row) presented the key to Mr. Hill as a memento.

A unique photograph taken at a match to mark the opening of Norwich Union's new pavilion at School Lane on 25th April 1959. Michael Falcon's "County" XI contained six players who had or were to captain Norfolk. They are, seated left to right, W. S. Thompson, W. J. Edrich, M. Falcon, P. G. Powell, L. A.  Barrett and second from the left in the back row D. G. Pilch. Among other Norfolk players in the side were J. C. Campbell-Gibson and B. G. W. Stevens, fifth and sixth from the left in the back row. The match, which was played on a new rubber-link matting wicket, saw Falcon declare at 140-6, then the home side reach 50-1 before rain prevented further play.

Edrich is Back!

AFTER the somewhat ordinary Fifties, the year 1960 proved a dramatic one for followers of Norfolk County Cricket Club. In 1959, Bill Edrich had returned from a glorious career with Middlesex to skipper his native county; and his inspired leadership had an immediate impact.

Edrich's team was well-balanced. Among those in the batting department were Henry Blofeld, a Cambridge blue who later found fame as a broadcaster, and Nigel Moore, who had played several games for Cambridge University in 1952. Unfortunately Moore had been at Cambridge when the University boasted a wealth of top players, including Peter May and David Sheppard, so had missed out on a blue. Reliable Ted Witherden, the former Kent player and Norfolk's only pro, had reached a record season aggregate for the County of 1031 runs (average 79.30) the previous season. In 1960 both he and Edrich would total in excess of 800 runs with averages of over 53.

Norfolk C.C. 1960. Back row, left to right: E. G. Witherden, D. C. Thorne, A. G. Coomb, G. G. Fiddler, J. J. Campbell-Gibson, H. C. Blofeld, L. W. J. Hart; Front row: P. G. Walmsley, P. G. Powell, W. J. Edrich, N. H. Moore, A. J. Corran

The strength of the bowling was demonstrated in the Lakenham match with Hertfordshire when medium fast bowler Arthur Coomb took 7-65 in the first innings and spinner David Thorne 7-48 in the second. Andrew Corran, who that season opened the bowling for the Gentlemen at Lord's, took most wickets, while that long-standing servant Peter Walmsley bagged his three hundredth wicket for the County against Nottinghamshire II at Newark. But it was Edrich who topped the bowling averages with 43 wickets at 16.16. Terry Allcock, the Norwich City forward, was a useful batsman and able wicket-keeper, with Blofeld deputising when he was not available.

Edrich's "do or die" approach was perhaps best typified in the match against Cambridgeshire at Lakenham, which brought a fourth successive victory. Having scored a 102 not out himself in Norfolk's first innings, Edrich eventually set Cambridge to score 215 in 172 minutes on the last afternoon - an inviting target. Cambridge made a sound start, but then crucial wickets tumbled, particularly that of Maurice Crouch who was spectacularly caught at backward short-leg by Ivan Watts, the brilliant Norwich Wanderers' fielder. As wickets began to fall, so did the drizzle, which then turned to rain with four batsman still remaining. But in true Edrich fashion, with Cambridgeshire entering into the spirit, the players

T. S. Hale bowled by Edrich during the Cambridgeshire second innings

stuck it out and the captain wound up the tail, finishing with 5-52. Amid scenes of great jubilation and car hooters sounding all round the ground, hordes of spectators rushed to the pavilion to cheer Edrich and his team off the field.

Bill Edrich leads the triumphant Norfolk players in at Lakenham in 1960 after beating Cambridgeshire - their fourth successive win

Norfolk finished top of the table and faced Lancashire II, the runners-up, in a Challenge Match at Lakenham. Disappointingly, this proved to be a big anticlimax. Lancashire's all-professional team, which included England bowlers Malcolm Hilton and Roy Tattersall, together with batsman Harry Pilling, who hit 79 not out in the first innings, proved too strong. Norfolk played well below their capabilities and lost by nine wickets - just as they had done against Yorkshire II in 1933. In the County's dismal second innings of 131, Tattersall claimed 5-17 with his off breaks, only Edrich with 43 offering any real resistance.

Edrich continued to lead the County in the Sixties with flair and example, but although there were magical times, nothing compared with 1960. W.J.'s first-class career is well-documented, but in two spells for Norfolk covering all matches he amassed 8308 runs and took 417 wickets, not to mention 154 catches, mostly taken at slip. In 1961, he scored two "not out" centuries in the Lakenham fixture with Staffordshire.

NORFOLK COUNTY CRICKET CLUB
MINOR COUNTIES CHAMPIONSHIP CHALLENGE MATCH
NORFOLK v. LANCASHIRE II. Wed., Thurs. & Fri., Sept. 7th, 8th & 9th, 1960
Times of Play :—First & Second Day—11-30 a.m. to 6-30 p.m. Third Day—11-30 a.m. to 6 p.m.

NORFOLK—1st. Innings		NORFOLK—2nd. Innings	
1 G. G. Fiddler b Booth	10	lbw b Tattersall	4
2 †H. C. Blofeld c Tebay b Hilton C.	4	b Booth	17
3 Witherden E. G. c Clayton b Hilton C.	6	b Hilton C.	0
4 N. H. Moore c Lever b Booth	27	lbw b Tattersall	23
5 *W. J. Edrich b Booth	18	c Bond b Tattersall	43
6 P. G. Powell b Tattersall	4	b Hilton C.	0
7 A. G. Coomb c Tattersall b Booth	24	b Tattersall	9
8 J. C. Gibson b Booth	5	c Clayton b Hilton M.	0
9 D. C. Thorne run out	16	c Hilton C b Hilton M.	2
10 A. J. Corran not out	11	c Collins b Tattersall	23
11 P. G. Walmsley b Tattersall	23	not out	0
Extras	5	Extras	10
Total	153	Total	131

	1	2	3	4	5	6	7	8	9	10	1	2	3	4	5	6	7	8	9	10
Wkts.																				
Runs	13	23	23	67	70	91	103	119	120	153	21	21	25	70	75	102	128	129	129	131

BOWLING ANALYSIS—First Innings.

	O	M	R	W		O	M	R	W
					Second Innings.				
Hilton C.	17	9	27	2		21	6	32	2
Lever	9	2	10	0		4	1	5	0
Collins	1	1	0	0					
Booth	22	9	63	5		23	8	57	1
Tattersall	16.5	4	48	2		30	22	17	5
					Hilton M.	10.2	5	10	2

LANCS.—1st. Innings		LANCS.—2nd Innings	
1 Bond J. c Witherden b Corran	12	not out	11
2 Booth B. b Walmsley	4	not out	46
3 Bolton A. c Coomb b Walmsley	1		
4 Tebay K. b Walmsley	0	lbw b Thorne	19
5 Collins R. c Blofeld b Corran	58		
6 ‡Clayton G. b Coomb	3		
7 Pilling H. not out	79		
8 *Hilton M. J. b Coomb	15		
9 Tattersall R. b Corran	6		
10 Lever P. b Walmsley	6		
11 Hilton C. c & b Corran	9		
Extras	13	Extras	3
Total	206	Total	79

	1	2	3	4	5	6	7	8	9	10	1	2	3	4	5	6	7	8	9	10
Wkts.																				
Runs	0	8	16	22	34	44	112	131	169	206	43									

BOWLING ANALYSIS—First Innings.

	O	M	R	W		O	M	R	W
					Second Innings.				
Walmsley	17	5	36	4		5	3	5	0
Corran	25.1	8	59	4		8.5	4	12	0
Coomb	24	6	62	2					
Thorne	15	6	36	0		7	0	33	1
					Edrich	8	2	26	0

*Captain. †Wicketkeeper. Umpires: W. E. Brown & S. H. Moore.
Score Card Threepence.   Toss Won by Lancashire

The Sixties did produce some fine home-grown players, notably wicket-keeper Doug Mattocks, all-rounder David Pilch, slow bowler Billy Rose, quickie Tracey Moore and Clive Radley, who played just one season before following in Peter Parfitt's steps to Middlesex. A personal highlight for Tracey Moore came in 1969 when Norfolk put up a admirable fight before losing a Gillette Cup match at Lakenham against mighty Yorkshire. Moore took 6-48, including the wickets of Hampshire, Padgett, Close and the "immovable" Boycott. Real Boy's Own stuff!

Norfolk players Evan Hall and Clive Radley both joined Middlesex in 1961. At the end of a one year contract Hall moved to a coaching appointment at Rugby public school for two years before returning to Norfolk. He played for Ingham, Dereham and Carrow

Michael Mason's XI at Castle Acre

A DELIGHTFUL series of annual matches took place in the 1960s between Castle Acre and star-studded XI's assembled by Michael Mason. They were staged at Castle Acre's ground, then on the Water Meadows. A pop group, trapeze artistes, the Singing Postman and Miss Roselyn from T.V.'s Romper Room were among a number of entertainers who attended these games, particularly to amuse spectators in the intervals. But the cricket was played in a serious vein.

Popular members of Mason's XI were Peter Parfitt and Clive Radley, then both with Middlesex. In the 1966 match, Radley scored 69 enabling Mason to declare at 168-9, and on a difficult wicket Castle Acre were dismissed for 72. Herbert Hargreaves, once a fast medium bowler with Yorkshire, took 6-32. It was Peter Parfitt who top-scored in 1968 when he made 82 in Mason's total of 212-9 declared. Parfitt received good support from Allan Watkins, the old Glamorgan all-rounder. A well-earned 49 not out by Mike Valentine saw Castle Acre respond with 182-6. But the results did not really matter. What did was the enjoyment of the crowd and the substantial sums raised for the Castle Acre club's funds.

Michael Mason (centre) with Peter Parfitt (left) and Clive Radley (right). Herbert Hargreaves stands behind

Batting for Mason's XI, Gerald Goodley (Norfolk) receives a ball from Charlie Wright, Algy Eagle is wicket-keeper. The batsman at the non-striking end is David Ling (Middlesex)

The Lord's Taverners Pull Them In at Ingham

The players at the match between a Norfolk XI and an Edrich XI in 1960 are, left to right, Ted Witherden, Tony Lock (Surrey), Henry Blofeld and Andy Seeley

MEET THE STARS . .
at a
GRAND CHARITY CRICKET MATCH
at
INGHAM CRICKET GROUND
ON STALHAM - SEA PALLING ROAD B1151 on
SUNDAY, SEPTEMBER 15th
at 1-30 p.m. (Gates Open at 12 noon)

AN ALL EDRICH XI.
Including: W. J. EDRICH, England and Middlesex, J. H. EDRICH, England and Surrey
V. THE
LORD'S TAVERNERS

Team to be selected from:

DENNIS COMPTON, England and Middlesex
ARTHUR PHEBEY, Kent (Captain)
ALEC BEDSER, England and Surrey
JIM LAKER, England and Essex
BEN BARNETT, Australia
ERIC BEDSER, Surrey
BILLY WRIGHT, England and Arsenal
JOHN WARR, England and Middlesex
JACK YOUNG, England and Middlesex

IAN CARMICHAEL, The Stage
TONY BRITTON, The Stage
RICHARD (Mr. Pastry) HEARNE, The Stage
JACK MARTIN, England and Kent
LEO BENNETT, Northants
WILLIE WATSON, England and Leicester
JON FELLOWES-SMITH, South Africa
WILLIAM FRANKLYN, The Stage
GRAHAM HILL, World Champion Racing Driver

ALL PROCEEDS TO THE
NATIONAL PLAYING FIELDS ASSOCIATION
Autograph Tent : Raffles : Teas : Refreshments
AMPLE CAR PARKS 2/6 CAR PARK ON GROUND 10/-
Admission to Ground by Programme Price 2/6

THE Sixties saw a series of wonderfully entertaining matches between the Edrich family XI and the Lord's Taverners. They were played on September Sunday afternoons on Ingham's delightful little tree-lined ground, which was invariably bathed in sunshine. Although these games may not have suited the cricket purist, they attracted huge crowds of up to 8000, who enjoyed the carnival cricket. With Bill captaining the family side, there were plenty of runs, wickets and exciting finishes. The results of the matches were largely immaterial, particularly as the Taverners often employed more than eleven batsman to achieve victory. But it was all great fun. The Taverners always included a galaxy of stars from the worlds of cricket and show business - and autograph hunters delighted in catching them! Many of the matches were in aid of the National Playing Fields Association and at the Ingham end were expertly organised by club secretary Andy Seeley, Jack "Bless Your Old Heart" Borrett and other officials.

Prior to the Taverners' first visit in 1963, the Edriches had played various representative XI's and it had been at Ingham in 1959 when the family suffered its first-ever reverse. With an injured Bill unable to bat and despite a lusty innings of 62 from Arthur, the Edrich XI lost to a Norfolk XI by 77 runs. The next year, with John scoring 171, they got their revenge, though Ingham's Andy Seeley scored a blistering 104 for the losers. The Edrich team, for whom W.J. scored 122, lost to Ted Witherden's team in 1961, but beat Jack Borrett's XI in 1962, when they reached their target of 220 for the loss of three wickets. The later match featured a first wicket stand of 180 by Brian and John for the family, and a lively third wicket partnership of 116 by Parfitt and Radley for Borrett's XI

Arthur Phebey, the Kent batsman who had hit 133 for Witherden's team in the 1961 match, assembled the Taverners' side; and for that first encounter in 1963 he pulled off a real coup - the late acquisition of Garfield Sobers. The great West Indian all-rounder arrived after a hectic journey from London, asleep in the back of a car after having had only one and a half hours in bed the night before. But he soon had the crowd wide awake, bowling John Edrich for six then producing an explosive innings of 62, which included two mighty sixes. One of these sailed high over the trees at the other end, nothing like it having been seen before on Ingham's little ground, which had seen more than its fair share of sixes. Using a bicycle to change positions at the end of each over, Richard "Mr Pastry" Hearne kept the crowd amused with comic interludes. After the match, Sobers had a hair-raising trip from Ingham back to the Waldorf Hotel in Central London. With racing-driver Graham Hill at the wheel, he got there in two hours!

Anglia T.V. broadcast the 1964 match in which W.J. and Brian both hit centuries in the family's total of 410-7 declared. But the day really belonged to ex-England captain Peter

The Lord's Taverners at Ingham in 1963. Arthur Phebey the captain is flanked by Gary Sobers and Graham Hill, with Richard Hearne at the front

The Edrich XI at the 1965 match. Back row, left to right: Fred, Jasper, Lyndon, George C., Peter G., Alan, Dudley; front row: Arthur E., Brian R., William J., George H., John, Geoffrey A., Midge

May and Basil D'Oliveira, who together launched a furious onslaught on the Edriches' bowling. After Ben Barnett, the former Australian Test player, had scored a century, May and D'Oliveira followed by putting on 200 in just over 40 minutes. Both scored "tons" in the Taverners' total of 413-10. There had been 823 runs and five centuries in four and a half hours!

David Frost turns to talk to Arthur Phebey as the Taverners take the field in 1965. Everton Weekes is on the left

Mr. Pastry" and Ernie Wise clown around at the 1967 match, while among those looking on are Clement Freud, Leslie Crowther, Jimmy Ellis (of 'Z' Cars fame) and David Frost. At the right cricketers Titmus, Radley and Parfitt watch the fun

In 1965, when John scored 143, the day's runs totalled 809 with the Taverners, who batted second, finishing on 404-10 and one run behind! Everton Weekes, another great West Indian, played in this match and he enjoyed a useful partnership with David Frost. Frost scored 33 and followed this up with 26 in 1967 when he opened the innings for the Taverners with Clive Radley. But it was 1966 which saw the highest number of runs for an Edriches versus Taverners fixture, when an incredible 856 were scored in four and a half hours for the loss of 21 wickets. The Taverners won with 12 wickets down and there had been 54 sixes!

Brian Edrich, who particularly seemed to make hay in these festive matches, hit 119 in 1967 and 150 in 1969. Great little knocks from show business stars in these particular years included Leslie Crowther's innings of 42 on the first occasion and Ian Carmichael's 36 on the second.

The last of this series of merry matches between the Edrich family XI and the Lord's Taverners was played in 1974, but it was those marvellous games of the mid-1960s that particularly stand out. It was truly a delightful privilege to have been at Ingham when they were played.

Chapter Six

A Glance at the Modern Game

Popular opening pair Stephen Plumb (left) and Carl Rogers walk out to open the innings in a Holt Cup match in 1991 against Suffolk which Norfolk won by nine wickets. In a Norfolk career which ran from 1978 to 1995, Plumb amassed over 10,000 runs for the County and twice scored two centuries in one match. His highest score was 204 not out against Cumberland in 1988, while in 1991 he topped the Minor Counties' batting averages with 992 runs at 90.18. An aggressive opening bat, Rogers has scored some fine centuries for Norfolk.

Some Personalities

APART from winning the Holt Cup knockout competition in 1986, recent Norfolk County sides have had little success in their quest for honours. There have been many disappointments, among them the one run defeat by Devon in a semi-final of the 1992 Cup competition and their failure to win the Minor Counties' Challenge Matches in 1981 and 1996. Appearances in the Nat West Trophy competition have seen some heavy defeats against first-class opponents, but the County were truly unfortunate to lose to Glamorgan in 1983 by 25 runs. A dubious leg-before decision against Parvez Mir, when he was going well on 37, swung the game Glamorgan's way. However, in spite of a lack of silverware, the last couple of decades or so have thrown up some great personalities.

Philip Sharpe (left), the former Yorkshire Test star, captained Norfolk between 1979 and 1982. With him at the front are all-rounder David Pilch (middle) and John Edrich, who returned from Surrey to play just one season for the County in 1979, the year this picture was taken. In Sharpe's absence, Edrich led the team to a fine six wicket win over the old enemy Suffolk, but in spite of an array of talent the County failed to secure a Gillette Cup spot.

In a career spanning the years from 1965 to 1989, faithful Robin Huggins scored 6883 runs for Norfolk at 27.64. His highest score was 110 which he made twice against Lincolnshire in 1981, when he was not out, and in 1987. His club cricket has been with Norwich Barleycorns, West Norfolk, Ingham, Downham and North Runcton. Recently he has been very much involved in the County club's administration, particularly on the cricket and selection side.

86

With an ice-pack on his bruised shin, popular Quorn (Fred) Handley sits it out at Vauxhall Mallards' Brundall ground. Perhaps he is reflecting on his past Minor Counties career (1969-1990) which saw him score 7800 runs for Norfolk with swashbuckling batting. Two innings typified his approach - 101 not out in 67 balls in a win against Cumberland in 1983 and a century before lunch in a win against Staffordshire in 1988.

Before the game with Durham in 1989, long-standing wicket-keeper Doug Mattocks was presented with a tankard to mark his 200th appearance for Norfolk. Having made his County debut in 1961, he retired from Minor Counties cricket in 1991 at the age of 47. He had claimed 459 victims (399 caught and 60 stumped) in his Norfolk career. He hit a century against Suffolk in 1966.

Enthusiastic pace bowler Rodney Bunting, whose local club cricket has been played with North Runcton, Ingham and Norwich Wanderers, took 201 wickets (average 21.00) for Norfolk either side of a first-class career with Sussex, for whom he played between 1988 and 1991. He made his Norfolk debut in 1985 and retired in 1995.

David Thomas powers in - a fearsome sight for any batsman. This picture (right) was taken around the time Thomas made his Norfolk debut in 1983 at the age of 20. In 1989 he received the Frank Edwards Trophy for the best bowling average (11.05) in the Minor Counties Championship that season. In 1994 the influential all-rounder topped the County's batting averages, scoring 461 runs at 76.83. He captained the County from 1991 to 1995.

Steve Goldsmith

All-rounder Steve Goldsmith joined Norfolk in 1993 and in his first season averaged 70 with the bat, scoring 917 runs. He and Roger Finney set a new County record for the third wicket with an unbroken stand of 290 against Cumberland. The aggressive Goldsmith reached 200 and ex-Derbyshire colleague Finney 107. In 1995 Goldsmith again topped the averages with 58.29. Finney, also a useful all-rounder, made his Norfolk debut in 1989 and retired in 1994 to become involved in coaching and the commercial side of the club

Roger Finney

Sponsorship and Top Competitions

WITH the emergence of two strong County leagues and a number of limited over knockout competitions, there has been an ever-increasing dependence on sponsorship in the last twenty-five years.

Bradenham made their debut in the Norfolk Alliance in 1977 and with this team took the Division II championship in 1989. The club had won the Boyle Cup way back in 1932 and the Mid-Norfolk Village Shield in 1937; and they used to change at the Lord Nelson pub, where tea was taken. A new pavilion was built in 1972 and since those days the club has made much progress. In 1993 Patrick Dewing (third from the left in the front row) followed in the footsteps of his father and grandfather by being elected club captain. The Norfolk Cricket Alliance, the first officially organised league embracing senior clubs right across the county, was founded in 1971. The first chairman was Peter Powell and Dereham were the first winners. In 1981, the year Andy Seeley became chairman, the league became the Norwich Union Norfolk Cricket Alliance and has enjoyed a happy relationship with the insurance giant ever since.

The Swardeston squad which won the Norfolk Cricket Alliance Premier League in 1988 after the village had fought its way to the top through the Divisions.

The squad are, back row, left to right: S. Taylor, C. Read, G. Tufts, M. Rayner, A. Lincoln, D. Thomas, J. Whitehead, S. Shearing, D. Bow-

ker; Front row: B. Howlett (scorer), J, Lund, R. Bradford, P. Thomas, N. Rudd, and D. Bassingthwaighte. Further successes followed and Swardeston are now one of the most powerful teams in the County.

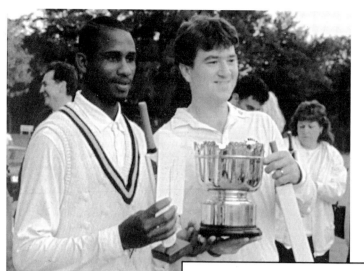

Man of the match Adrian Braithwaite, one of the Vauxhall Mallards' West Indian stars, and skipper Robbie Garrett with the Stan Biss Trophy after the Mallards had beaten Horsford in the 1992 final on their home ground of Brundall. In 1995, with Garrett scoring 72, Mallards took the Bob Carter Cup for the first time

With young Robert Moyser, the former Diss batting prodigy scoring 98 not out, Vauxhall Mallards stormed to victory in the 1996 Bob Carter Challenge Cup Final. The 60 over knockout competition was the brainchild of Eric Bedwell, a former R.A.F. Coltishall and Cromer C.C. player, and took off in 1969 when Dereham were the first winners.

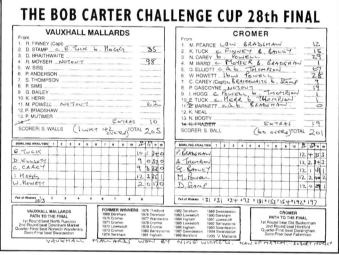

While his Alliance future was being clarified in 1996, former Pakistan player Parvez Mir turned out for the Norfolk League Division Five outfit Hardingham! He is seen here with Les King (centre), the League's sponsor and Hardingham president, and Andy Gardiner, the village club's big hitter who hammered the League's record score of 223 not out. The Norfolk Cricket League evolved from the Norfolk Cricket Federation and had been sponsored by Olympic Removals.

Short Singles!

VISCOUNT Coke (second from the left) after he had presented the Holkham Cricket Club with a new pavilion in 1982. Among others in the picture are Richard Foulds, Holkham's captain, and Ian Whitworth, who skippered the Vice-Presidents' XI, which played the club side in a celebratory match. Formerly the players changed in "The Potting Shed", an old wooden hut

It was President's Day at Vauxhall Mallard's Brundall ground when this picture was taken in 1990. What a team it was that turned out for President Stan Biss. Flanking the President are Clive Lloyd and Imran Khan, former West Indies and Pakistan captains. Seated next to Imran is Norfolk's own Quorn Handley. Parvez Mir is behind Mr. Biss.

The Norfolk Junior Cup has survived in the changing cricket world and its centenary was celebrated in 1991. In that year Vauxhall Mallards A beat Sprowston A in the final at Old Buckenham. Brian Broom, Mallard's captain, is pictured with Jill Miller, the Sheriff of Norwich, who had just presented him with the cup. In a sporting contest, Broom's men made 137-9, while Sprowston could only manage 123, despite a fine knock of 76 by man of the match Ashlea Blyth.

Star footballer Chris Sutton tries out his batting stance during a charity match at Hellesdon High School in 1995. The match was staged to raise funds towards cricket nets for the school. On the previous Saturday, Sutton, a good striker of the ball, had hit a century in 81 minutes for Drayton against Yare C.C. in a King's Norfolk League Division Two match.

Paul Prichard (left) and John Lund, Old Buckenham's experienced captain, out in the middle for the toss before the day-night floodlit encounter between Prichard's Essex XI and the village in 1996. This match and the previous one the year before against Northamptonshire were an innovation for followers of Norfolk cricket. The games were in aid of benefits for Northant's Nick Cook and Prichard.

Peter Free plays resolutely forward in Old Buckenham's match at the end of the 1996 season against Norwich Wanderers. Tim Boon is in the slips, while the wicket-keeper is Gareth Hopkins, the New Zealand Under 19s player. Hopkins scored a ton in Wanderer's win. Boon enjoyed a superb season with Norfolk in 1996, scoring 902 Championship runs, including four centuries, at 64.43

Investing in Youth

THE last few years have seen great strides in the development of youth coaching and competition within the County. The creation of the Norfolk Youth Cricket Coaching Scheme in 1984 has given added impetus and over 40 clubs now run youth teams.

The great Sir Garfield Sobers spoke at the Gresham's School 1st XI dinner prior to the team's first visit to Barbados in 1993. The school has now made three visits to Barbados for the Sir Gary Sobers International Schools Festival.

Former Test favourite Derek Randall coaching two youngsters at Saxlingham in 1995. Randall was in the village to christen a new all-weather wicket, two practice nets and a bowling machine.

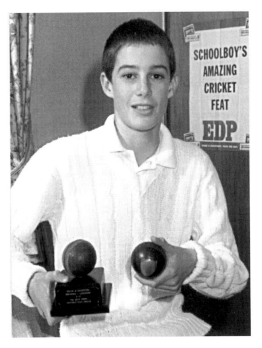

Nick Causton, aged 14, attracted the attention of the national media when he took six wickets in six successive deliveries playing for Brooke against Loddon in the Rubens Hales Youth League in 1996. He thus emulated his great-grandfather, who was mentioned earlier, and is seen holding the balls by which they achieved their respective feats

The Evergreens

THE annual Evergreens' match has been a popular event on the Norfolk cricket calendar ever since the first one was staged in 1974. The teams are comprised of Golden Oldies from around the County who are over 50. There is no upper age limit! In that very first game, Fred Barnard's XI made 90, a score which was comfortably passed by Eddie Symond's team for the loss of five wickets. Norman Brighton and George Howard each hit 23 runs for the losers, while Neville Yellop top-scored with 39 for the winners.

Cyril Rowe batting in the very first Evergreens' match. The fielder facing is Neville Yellop and the wicket-keeper Eddie Symonds.

A happy group of Evergreens in 1994.

The Evergreens' match has also been played at Bradenham, Dereham, Great Witchingham and in recent years at Swardeston. The Black Sheep Cricket Club, founded several years ago, is made up of veteran players and raises money for local charities. A leading light has been Barry Battelley, the former Dereham stalwart. Evergreen and Black Sheep players just love the game of cricket. They themselves are part of Norfolk's cricketing heritage.

Norfolk Takes On The World!

THE 1996 Lakenham Festival came to a splendid climax when a Norfolk Select XI, including guest players Neil Foster, Graeme Fowler and Wayne Larkins, took on a star-studded Rest of the World XI, captained by Richie Richardson, in a 55 over challenge match. With the likes of Alvin Kallicharran, Keith Arthurton, Jimmy Adams and Javed Miandad in the World team, the game gave local cricket followers the opportunity to watch some of the big names of the game.

Kallicharran, who made a somewhat pedestrian start but later opened up, scored 67 for the World XI, who totalled 238. Keith Arthurton chipped in with a breezy 64, while Norfolk bowling honours went to Tim Boon and Steve Goldsmith, who bagged three economical wickets apiece. With the awesome Ian Bishop in the opposition's attack, Norfolk's task was not easy, but a sound 59 from Boon kept the score ticking along and eventually skipper Paul Newman (36 not out) saw the County home by two wickets off the last ball in a nail-biting finish. The cricket may not have met with the approval of traditionalists, but it was a most wonderful day for the biggest crowd seen at Lakenham for years.

Richie Richardson surrounded by autograph hunters as he leads out the World XI.

Part of the large crowd at Lakenham watching the Norfolk Select XI match against the Rest of the World XI in 1996.

ACKNOWLEDGEMENTS

I wish to record my special thanks to Bryan Stevens, who kindly gave me access to his Norfolk County records and other material, and to Pat Freeman, who loaned scrapbooks compiled by Len Hart, her late father. The staff of the Norfolk Studies Library, King's Lynn Library and the Norfolk Record Office have all been most helpful.

Among many others, who have either lent photographs or offered snippets of information, I should especially like to mention: D. Bates • Jack Borrett • G. Burrows • Andrew Buxton • Paul Cattermole • Mrs. C. Harmer • Jeremy Cozens-Hardy • A. Curzon • John Dewing • G. Dyball • Eddie Dye • Arthur Edrich • W. Fisher • Richard Fryer • Les Heyhoe • B. Howling • Les King • Mrs. M. Lister • C. Loome • Ray Lusted • Mrs. J. Magrath • Mr. J. J. Magrath • Michael Mason • Mrs. E. Mason • Fred Masters • Mr H. Nunn • David Osborne • C. Piper • Canon M. K. Raikes • Dr. P. Rawlence • Andy Seeley • Stephen Skinner • Eddie Symonds • Cedric Thistleton-Smith • S. Taylor • K. Thompson • David Turner • Miss Vera Watson • A. Webster • A. A. Wilson • Roger Wilson • Mrs I. Worman • Bradenham C.C. • Garboldisham C.C. • Hillington C.C. • Old Buckenham C.C. • Sandringham C.C. • Norwich School • Thetford Grammar School

Many other clubs and individuals have loaned photographs and I am grateful for their help.

Special acknowledgement must be given to the following, whose photographs I have reproduced with their kind permission:

Andrew Coe: 67, 71b, 83a, 84a
Eastern Counties Newspapers: 4, 68a, 69b, 71a, 75a, 79a, 79b, 84b, 86a, 89b, 91a, 93a, 94a
Gressenhall Rural Life Museum: 5, 15b
Lynn News: 69c, 81a, 81b
M.C.C. Collection: 9, 10a, 10b, 11b
Norfolk County Cricket Club: 14a, 15a, 55a
Norfolk Library & Information Service: 9a
Norfolk Record Office: 12b (Acc Castle Museum 30/1/73)
Norwich Union: 74b, 77b
Roger Mann Collection: 6b, 14b

I have endeavoured to trace all copyright holders and if I have not contacted anyone please accept my apologies.

My very special thanks must go to the great John Edrich for writing such a splendid foreword. I would also like to thank Richard Barham for reading the text, Terry Burchell for photographic work and my wife Wendy and daughter Joanne for word-processor duties and bearing with me whilst this work was researched and compiled.

BIBLIOGRAPHY

Cricketing references in Norwich Newspapers 1701-1800 (J. S. Penny)
Files of the Eastern Daily Press, Diss Express, Lynn News, Norfolk Chronicle and Norwich Mercury
Norfolk C.C. Handbooks and Reports - various years
Norfolk Cricket Annual (Jarrolds) 1889-1898
Norfolk Cricket Annual (C. B. L. Prior) 1909-11
Norfolk Cricket Annual (R. Borret and R. G. Pilch) 1926 -27
Wisden Cricketers' Almanack - various years